MW00476328

Stilettos in the rearview

LAUREN NELSON

Copyright 2022 by Lauren Nelson

All rights reserved. International copyright secured. No part of this book may be reproduced, stored in a retrieval system, or transmitted in any form or by any means electronic, mechanical, photocopying, recording, or otherwise—without the prior written permission of New Netherland Press and Lauren Nelson, except for the inclusion of brief quotations in an acknowledged review.

ISBN: 978-0-93-766662-3

Cover design by Shawna Serpe

New Netherland Press
Schenectady, NY

Dedication

To my son Daniel. It's funny how the roles have shifted and YOU have become MY biggest supporter. There are no words for how much I love you.

To Shawna, the sister I chose, who helped bring color and flair into my book and continues to bring the same into my life daily. We may not share blood, but no matter, what we share is much more important.

To Mommom. Thank you for always believing in me and for always being proud of me. I will forever hear the way that you called me "Darling" with so much sincere love that the word itself was the emotion incarnate.

To JS for your input and definitions, but more importantly for inspiring me to seek for and realize the strength in my own heart. You unknowingly challenged me to achieve one of the largest pieces of my growth thus far.

Chapter One

Raton Pass

I may have bitten off more than I can chew, the agonizing thought in my mind. I swiftly wiped the sweat from my palm onto the leg of my jeans. Drying one hand at a time with the other grasping so tightly I could feel the pulse from my hand against the smooth surface of the steering wheel.

I see a small pull-off in a construction zone. Nobody's there but I can stop and catch my breath. I've never heard of a mountain pass before and my paralyzing fear of heights was getting the better of me. It was just the fifth day of my solo cross-country journey and this challenging piece of highway taking me from Raton, New Mexico, into Trinidad, Colorado, just might be where it ends.

I'd already survived a near kidnapping in Memphis and witnessed the police chase that followed a shooting in Arkansas. Now I'm faced with the sheer drop-offs of the Raton Pass. Parked in the narrow gravel on the edge of the road, I consider calling 911 to have rescue come retrieve me from this mountain and take me to the nearest airport. I can ship my Chevy pickup home. Just then a small, four-door sedan with a group of collage-age girls pulled up next to me.

I watch through my passenger window as the giggling girls jump out of their Toyota, race through a Chinese fire drill, and jump back into their car to take on the intimidating and dramatic mountain pass. Now I know I have to press on. I am just a one-hour drive from my friend Lucy and her beautiful mountain refuge. I've been looking forward to seeing Lucy since she moved to Colorado from Pennsylvania earlier this year, and I sure didn't set out on this cross-country sojourn to quit on day five!

I took a deep breath and pulled back onto Highway 25, in the left lane as far from the cliffside as possible. Going 40 miles an hour with my flashers on, head pounding and tears streaming down my cheeks, I made it over the summit and crossed the Colorado state line.

The Colorado visitor center was a truly welcome sight. I put my truck in park and rested my forehead against my hands, having not yet loosened my death grip on the steering wheel. I sat there for several minutes, shaking. Gathering myself, I got out of the truck and made my way inside.

As I exited the ladies' room into the visitor-center lobby, which was bright with sunlight streaming in through the glass walls, I scanned the room for any sign of empathetic people who might possibly be able to sense the ordeal that I had just been through. I needed human interaction. A kind couple, Mary and Jake, noticed me and asked if I was ok. I suppose it was apparent that I was not feeling fantastic. They empathized with me about the experience. Mary and Jake have lived in Colorado for a while, they moved from the East and recounted their first time over the pass as well. They gave me good information and sound advice, and validated my feelings by telling me that many people have trouble with that particular part of the road. It helped. After several minutes of conversation, I thanked them, we exchanged information, then parted ways.

I was alone again, this time feeling grateful for the freedom of peaceful reclusion and a satisfying sense of accomplishment. I made my exit through the heavy glass doors of the building, finally able to appreciate the beauty of the Rockies now filling my vision.

I found myself standing on the sidewalk outside the southern wall of the building. In front of me a rustic post-and-rail fence did the important job of protecting me from taking a dangerous wrong step. I was informed by a plaque: "Trinidad Colorado visitor center built 1986, elevation of 6480 feet above sea level."

Looking up from the plaque and across the vastness, I took in the magic all around me: A spectacular view of the majestic mountain range. It was that moment when it is still daylight but the sun is preparing itself for its evening descent. The shift is palpable. The light of the setting sun wrapped the stone peaks in an orange glow, pouring its warm rays onto my skin, rejuvenating me. I closed my eyes and soaked it in. Though labored because of the altitude, I breathed in the fresh, clean Colorado mountain air.

The last light of dusk finds me on the dirt frontage road outside of Pueblo, Colorado. The backdrop of the snow-capped Rocky Mountains in the distance behind the rolling hills of lush green looked like a painting. I admired the roaming cows with their calves grazing all around me, only cattle grates in the pavement preventing the herd from wandering onto the main road, and more grates stopping their entry onto the interstate.

I navigated my truck onto Lucy's gravel driveway. I followed it for a half a mile through hills and turns filled with unfamiliar vegetation, so different from what grows in the east. Happiness welled up inside of me when I saw my good friend standing outside of her beautiful log home, waiting for me as I turned into the pull-off made for her pick up truck (most of the girls in my world drive trucks) to the open area next to it.

I was clearly war-torn. In her attempt to comfort me, Lucy was my therapeutic listening ear wrapped up in an adorable, compassionate, brilliant blonde package.

She had a nourishing fresh meal prepared which we enjoyed while taking in the awe-inspiring view through her wall of picture windows. The scenery would be even more spectacular in the morning when daylight would proudly expose the expansive, boundless landscape from Lucy's back deck and the noble summit of the colossal Greenhorn Mountain standing watch in the distance.

I didn't know where to begin my story or how to put it together. My initial rambling seemed like senseless, disorganized babbling to me, but then the story of the last five days started coming together. It became apparent that everything so far has lined up as though I was being helped, as though I were being guided. Everything from my narrow escape in Memphis to the carload of girls who pulled up next to me, making me realize I had to persevere.

Chapter 2

Will the Real Jessi Northwood Please Stand Up

A few months earlier…

"That's crazy," I said to him. "Shouldn't you be thinking about your future, your retirement?" Our conversation reverberated over glassware clinking and the low drone of voices in the background.

"Promise me you're going to wake up tomorrow," he responded with confidence, without hesitation. "Guarantee me you're going to see your retirement. Maybe you'll be here that long, maybe you won't." Jesse's point was beginning to sink in.

"Do you really want to wait until you're 65 or 70 to begin living? If you do make it that long, will you be able to enjoy life and all of the experiences it has to offer in the same way as now, while you are still young? You need to live now!"

Still young I thought, I guess it's relative. Here I am, a woman in the final year of my 40's, staring 50 in the face. After raising a child to be a successful adult, contrasted by a slew of unsuccessful, painful relationships and working more hours than should be considered healthy, am I still young? Well, I'm active; I dance, run, ride horses, hike and I still choose to see attractiveness when I look in the mirror. I suppose I am still young.

My friend, who has the exact same first and last name as I do (with the exception of replacing the "i" in Jessi for an "e"), made a great point. His message was beginning to alter my view. I'm lacking balance. I tend to play it safe. I always have. Stashing for a future and all those things we are conditioned to believe are most important. I felt spending money on myself was entirely selfish and taking time off of work was just plain irresponsible.

Memories of hearing about Jesse back in our teen years fluttered through my thoughts. There were two high schools in our district. He went to Harriton High, while I attended Lower Merion High School. We had several mutual friends yet we never met each other during those years. I had no way of knowing that he would turn out to be possibly my most life-changing friend. I finally met

Jesse my first time at a local members-only nightclub. Amongst the pounding techno music and flashing, hypnotic dance-floor lights, I carefully filled out a pink membership application. The forms were separated: yellow for the men and pink for the women.

Once I finished my application and handed it to the overly muscled bouncer who stood expressionless like the Queen's guards at Buckingham Palace, I entered. The nightclub was located in the lower level of a shopping center. It had a basement feel complete with a faint moldy smell. Toward the back of the large open room was a small, fenced area with a well-worn wooden parquet dance floor, discolored from years of drunken bar-goers dancing the night away.

The logical first stop was to find myself a drink, so I made my way to the bar. I squeezed through the sweaty sea of people, peeling my feet off the sticky, beer-stained carpet with each step. When the bartender finally noticed me, I ordered my go-to vodka cranberry. Out of the corner of my eye I could see a heavyset, middle-aged woman wearing black cargo pants and an unflattering yellow polo shirt attempting to get my attention. As she got closer, I realized she was a club employee. She quickly positioned herself beside me at the bar. "Miss, you filled out the wrong application, you should've filled out the pink, not the yellow," she informed me.

"I did fill out the pink! Let me see that...", I replied with confusion.

I couldn't believe it! Jesse is here! "That's not my application, that's the other Jesse Northwood," I corrected her. He was here! I scurried away from the woman and hastefully searched through the energized crowd, asking random strangers if they knew Jesse Northwood until after what felt like ages, someone pointed him out to me.

Navigating my way through the crowded room, careful in my haste not to cause any spilled drinks or step on any feet, I quickly rehearsed in my mind what I would say.

I was so excited! I spotted Jesse standing in a small group of his friends, not really noticing that he was quite a good-looking guy. I introduced myself as he stood with his charming smile and athletic build. I knew he would be just as thrilled to meet me. Well, I sure was wrong.

Jesse looked at me with what seemed like slight annoyance and an untrusting sideways glare then simply said, "No, I don't know what you're talking about." He went immediately back to mingling with his friends, turning away from me, not looking back. This reaction quickly crushed the joy of finally knowing my name twin. I walked away, embarrassed and disenchanted. I would not see Jesse again for 25 years.

It was not the right time to know him. I truly think if Jesse had been in my life at that time, he may not have had the impact on me that he had all these years later. The right time for him to be in my life was not until now.

"Another round?" The bartender's words snapped me back from my nostalgic daydream. I was no longer surrounded by the colorful dancing lights of the dimly lit, dingy 90's nightclub. Instead, I found myself in the present time at the Great American Pub in Wayne, Pennsylvania, with its rustic wooden interior and pine-green accents giving it the atmosphere of a classic Irish pub. Jesse sat on the barstool beside mine with his kind, concerned eyes fixed on me. His eyes were scanning my face for any tell-tale sign that I was absorbing what he was trying to get across to me. I pondered, barely noticing the faint undertone of the ESPN commentators in the background. He was right. I had to find balance between responsibility and enjoyment of life.

So, I planned to take my trip. I picked a start date and marked it in my calendar.

I thought it would be a once-in-a-lifetime trip, however what I would later learn is that it would be the doorway to so much more.

Chapter 3

To Plan or Not to Plan

Having contemplated all of the places that I desired visiting, I realized there were many, many places and people that I wanted to see. I wanted to go to unfamiliar cities to dance in honky-tonks where I didn't know anybody. I wanted to get back to Boise, Idaho, where I spent a short amount of time last year at Dirt Road Dancing for country swing dance lessons. I wanted to go dance in Phoenix with a group that's well known because of a viral YouTube video which had been circulating for years amongst the dance community. The group in Phoenix was very responsive to me through social media messages in the past and made it known to me that I would be welcome there.

I wanted to visit my friend Tess in Dallas. I wanted to see my horse friends in Florida. I wanted to dance my way across the country and back. Soon the trip evolved from a short, two-week jaunt to Nashville and Colorado to a life-changing month-and-a-half of a loosely planned cross-country adventure. It became real when I scheduled four days of dance lessons with Elise and Troy at Dirt Road Dancing. I was committed now; it was really going to happen.

The whimsical flexibility required for this kind of a journey must be juxtaposed against the reality of the person I was before; rigid, scheduled, ruled by my perfectly structured calendar, rarely deviating to stop and smell the roses–let alone wander mountain trails and backcountry roads through the Midwest.

Spontaneity was unfamiliar to me. Since the tender age of 21 I had been a mother. My life revolved around my child's needs and the pressures of work. After years of doing whatever jobs I could find and a long stretch of tending bar, I finally discovered my niche and subsequently became a massage therapist. I started my own small business thinking it would give me more freedom. I learned instead that my work ethic was intense and incorruptible.

Previously, when I had to find work in movie theaters, day care centers, and bartending, I was not as focused. The goal was simply to provide for my little boy and make ends meet. The process of becoming a massage therapist and managing clients did help me to organize my life, though to a fault.

Every minute of every day was planned. Once an event or task was on the calendar it was in stone in my mind and could not be changed without causing severe anxiety. It felt as though one thing out of order would throw everything else off. Time off and vacations were things other people did.

Slowly over the last three years I learned to take a couple of days off here, a week off there. I thought that meant that I was really in the process of getting my feet wet, so to speak, in the context of travel and basic selfcare. I suppose I was beginning to figure it out even before Jesse's words catapulted me to a new level of understanding.

One thing that I was recently able to do that I had never been able to do before was remove myself from a relationship that was unfulfilling and at times verbally abusive. I tended to hold on to things that were bad for me because the idea of loss or abandonment was too scary and painful to endure. My longest non-relationship, as one friend called it, was a thirteen-year sunken investment.

I often compared myself in this relationship to an elegant pair of designer red stilettos. They look stunning when I take them out and put them on. They make me feel glamorous when I go out wearing them. What the observer does not know is that they are quite uncomfortable and definitely not my first choice for regular wear. Thus, I rarely take them out. Instead, I keep them in a box in my closet for special occasions. When I want them, they are there, I can rely on that. They're mine and nobody else can touch them although I don't give them very much of my time or attention. When I do want them, I take them out, I wear them, I get numerous compliments. When I'm done with them I put them away in the box knowing they'll be there when I desire them next, which almost certainly won't happen for a good while. I may not want much time with them but nobody else can touch them because they're mine. That is how I saw myself in this relationship, I was to him as my red stilettos were to me.

I was overwhelmingly lonely in that relationship. I didn't mind the idea of being alone but being alone without the possibility of love while bound to a commitment-less commitment was excruciating.

When I finally got the strength to walk away from the Red Stiletto Guy, I was no longer lonely. I was free. It was my first step towards unbinding myself from all the things that did not bring me joy in my life and looking for the things that did. I suppose this is why I was ready to hear and able to digest what Jesse had to say to me in the pub.

I decided that I wanted my trip as unconstrained and off-the-cuff as I had never been. If I was going to be impetuous, then I was going all out! I would plan only a starting destination of Nashville and a date to arrive in Boise.

I have friends in Nash and I know the dancing scene there, an easy start. I know I will have fun with Tina and Randy, some of my dancing friends living in Music City who I met on a previous weekend trip there last year. I will probably continue on to Colorado after that, but whatever happens in-between I will leave up to fate. Then I won't have anywhere to be until June for my dance lessons in Boise. I was willing to take a chance that it would all turn out OK and that I would find hotel rooms and if I didn't find a room I was prepared for sleeping in my truck which would be fine with me. I stocked my truck with blankets, pillows, water and camping meals for just such impromptu state of affairs. I picked May 22 as the day I would leave home in the direction of Tennessee and then I guessed at a round-about time that I would likely make it to Colorado. I checked with both Lucy in Pueblo, Colorado, and Christine in Moffat, Colorado, to see if they would be around. They each said get here when you can and please give a day or two notice. These girls are both horse friends from Pennsylvania that made their way to living in Big Sky country.

Chapter 4

...and She's Off

I have one more massage to do and then I can take off! While getting ready to leave work, go home for a quick bite and load the truck, I noticed that the back of my iPhone broke. Frustration fluttered through my senses as I had no idea how that happened and no time to go to Apple. "Oh well," I thought, "At least I didn't break a bone like I normally do every time I try to leave town." Shortly after arriving home and kicking off my shoes (I am adamant about no shoes in the house), as if on cue in an absurd play, my little toe struck a chair leg. Dread shot through me as did the searing pain. Is this seriously the way my dream trip is starting? I lamented.

Injuries like broken bones are weird events that plague many of my adventurous endeavors. Troubleshooting, problem solving, clearing obstacles. These are all things I have determined to do as I move forward to make this trip not only happen but be enjoyed! I called the Apple store in Nashville and set up an appointment for a replacement on Monday. They were most accommodating which made me optimistic about the first leg of this journey. One problem solved.

I hit the road. Although originally planning the western route, my GPS kept insisting I take the southern route. Figuring that the GPS knew better than I did about the traffic situation, I went along with this plan only to find a frustrating jam en route only minutes after leaving home. After finally getting through that hold up, I found another block near Delaware and another entering Maryland.

"Seems I'm going to be hitting a lot of traffic jams," I reasoned out loud. I settled in for the long ride and figured on trying to get as close to Tina and Randy's as possible tonight and finish the stretch to Nashville in the morning.

Clearly off to a great start: broken phone, maybe broken toe, miles of taillights blocking my way, finally a sight to warm my heart: The billboard "Welcome, Virginia is for Lovers." After all that the day had challenged me with, it seemed astounding that I had finally gotten to Winchester, Virginia, where I stopped for fuel. What could possibly go wrong? I should have known better than to tempt the fates with this thought.

Gasoline spraying all over the side of my truck was not the sweet Southern welcome I had hoped for. I quickly let go of the pump handle realizing this pump is broken and gas is leaking out from everywhere, yet somehow not a drop got on me. I went inside, informed the uninterested cashier about the debacle. He ignored me, his thumbs moving rapidly over the screen of his smartphone. Walking back to my truck, rather irked, I moved to a different pump and continued fueling up. I climbed back into the driver's seat and put my new lip gloss on. My lips were dry and I was going to enjoy this new raspberry shade.

Truck tank full, fresh cup of coffee, and glossed lips, I re-entered the road feeling revitalized. Continuing my drive, now on Interstate 81, I start to feel my throat getting tight. Now it's getting really tight. As I reach for my Benadryl and my EpiPen I backtrack in my head what I had eaten that would've caused an allergic reaction. With an EpiPen in hand prepared to do whatever I need to do, I realized the only thing I had touched was that brand-new lip gloss. Being allergic to red dye I always buy all-natural but what I should've bought was vegan (I promise, you don't want to know what is in red dye that makes it natural but not vegan). Looking at the label I see that there's red food dye called carmine in the all-natural lip gloss. Benadryl is helping, after ten minutes it started to get better and after thirty it was much better. I carefully stowaway my EpiPen for future use.

It's a long drive through Virginia, so I stopped at Dunkin' Donuts for a coffee and the guy at the counter gave it to me for free. I have no idea why but I'll just assume he was nice. I started to get tired about 8:15 PM and it wasn't even dark yet. I really wanted to keep going but even the coffee wasn't waking me up. I figured I either need to sleep, or dance! I called John, another dancing friend from the home of the Grand Ole Opry. John is a wiz at finding random boot-stomping dance halls. "I'm outside of Roanoke, can you help me find somewhere to dance?" I asked him. My thought was, dance for an hour to re-energize and then hit the road again. John did his research, called me back after discovering a place called Sidewinders in Roanoke.

Sidewinders was only an eight-minute drive from where I was. Exit 143 was coming up very quickly, I worked my way to the right lane and steered my truck onto the off-ramp. As I drove away from the familiar highway I had my first moment of slight discomfort. I didn't know the area and I had a pang of nerves that I quickly pushed away. This was what the trip was supposed to be new places, people and adventures. I arrived at the club and found a parking spot right in front of the bar, as if it was meant to be.

I asked the bouncer at the front door who the regular dancers were. He directed me to a table with a group of young, pretty girls and a few bearded young guys in cowboy hats who were all probably half my age. I confidently approached the table and while already pulling out a chair I asked them if they would mind if I joined them. Without hesitation the whole gang chimed in with approval allowing this newcomer to partake in the festivities. I filled them in on who I was, where I was from and what I was doing there; in return they shared their stories with me.

Although looking somewhat young for my 49 years I couldn't imagine that they were incognizant of the significant generation gap, yet they were as welcoming and inviting as if I were always one of their coterie.

After a short stint of line dancing with my new comrades, to my surprise and pleasure, I noticed a couple on the dance floor doing a fabulous swing dance. Her auburn hair was flying around her as he spun her and dipped her with impeccable precision. The dance concluded with a flawless dip and I dashed over to compliment them, and to ask her if I might "borrow" her husband for a dance. Turns out they dance in Arizona, and I was familiar with the style as I had been following that group of Phoenix dancers online. What were the chances of finding members of such a well-known and talented group right here in this rustic Virginia honky-tonk? The wife granted me the dance and he obliged. I thoroughly enjoyed his lead style and after the dance I thanked the couple and made my way to the table where my new young friends welcomed me back. They were nursing their fruity, colorful drinks and laughing over some joke that was set within a youthful pop-culture context. Chuckling to myself, not understanding the reference didn't phase me, my smile remained and took another sip of my bourbon.

A short while later I stood watching the dancers zig and zag and turn about the floor. I daydreamed of the numerous nights ahead, imagining what wonderful surprises they might hold when I realized someone was trying to get my attention. A very attractive, tall man, most likely in his mid-30's, wearing an orthopedic boot on one leg, introduced himself as Alex and asked me for a dance. My mind tried to work out how the heck he was going to accomplish the task but having been taught to never turn down a dance, I accepted. Wow, this guy has moves, I marveled, broken foot and all!

If I had not asked the Arizona couple for a dance, Alex would never have known I knew how and would not have asked me. Line dancers dominated the floor that night so there was no reason to assume any of us would know how to swing dance. It's funny how things lined up for me this evening. I felt like a princess at the ball as Alex spun me around the floor for the remainder of the evening.

After several hours at Sidewinders, rather than the one hour I originally planned on staying, my striking young dance partner suggested we take a rest and have a drink. He bought me a Basil Hayden neat (my current go-to, having graduated over the years from vodka and cranberry to bourbon) and himself a Bud Light. We sat with tired legs and light hearts enjoying our drinks. I was becoming slightly distracted by Alex's sparkling light brown eyes.

I learned that Alex had broken his foot through an unfortunate incident with a bear. Three weeks earlier while on vacation visiting his friend, Ken in Oregon, the two guys were on the patio watching Ken's daughter play in the yard and reminiscing on all the years that had passed since they saw each other last. Amid the old friend's laughter over a memory of a drunken ski trip gone bad, a bear cub wandered out from the surrounding brush. It was approaching the unsuspecting playful girl as she stacked her blocks and maneuvered her stuffed animals, pretending to be a zookeeper.

Adrenaline pumping, Ken and Alex jumped to action and ran with all they had in them. Alex, being marginally more fit than Ken, was first to arrive at the girl's side. Without hesitation or a thought for his own safety, nothing but his own body as a weapon, he kicked it. That's what happened, he kicked the bear! The impact broke Alex's foot but thankfully the cub scurried off. This action prevented mama bear from coming to search for her offspring in Ken's yard and the little girl lived to play zookeeper another day.

As gripping as his story was, I found myself fighting to pay attention to Alex's words rather than to his muscular arms and handsome features. I was also taking note that the part of me that becomes captivated with a good-looking man is still intact, it was merely in temporary hibernation.

I hated to say goodbye to my new young friend, but I had to get back on the road if I wanted to get anywhere near Nashville before the morning. Alex walked me to my truck, opened the driver side door for me verifying the chivalrous gentleman breed was alive and well. We exchanged information so that we could keep in touch and have more dances in the future.

My time at Sidewinders had given me a good shot of energy so I was recharged enough to drive about another hour or two closer to Nashville before I got tired again. I found a 24-hour Love's truck stop and climbed into the backseat of my truck in an attempt to get some sleep. After only two hours of shut eye I woke up, the backseat of the Silverado much less comfortable than I could have imagined. I drove another two hours before I got exhausted a third time. I found another truck stop, this one a BP, much cleaner and I was able to get another two hours of sleep before the sun came up insisting that I move it along.

Chapter 5

Nashville and Beyond

The time in Nashville went pretty much as expected: wonderful. I've been there several times before and enjoy it equally well each time. Staying with Randy and Tina is always fun. During the day Tina and I sat in the lush emerald grass of their sizable backyard soaking in the sun and catching up. Girl talk is always so satisfying to the soul. The nights were made for dancing. Country swing, otherwise known as Cowboy swing, is our sweet obsession. Tina, Randy, John and I wander between the Wildhorse Cafe and the famous Jason Aldean bar on Broadway in downtown Nashville where we can let loose, dip and spin till our hearts' content. It was one wonderful full night of dancing. I had a good night's rest and in the morning I was ready to move forward onto the next chapter of my adventure.

Nashville is about where my comfort level sits, traveling to states unknown to me beyond Tennessee is brand-new territory for me. It's also brand new for me to be away from home for more than five or six days at a time. I've never taken this kind of time off of work. Although I had come to terms with the idea of this extended time off, I still felt as though I was doing something wrong. I felt guilty although I had covered all of my bases. My cat Oliver was being cared for by someone I trust implicitly. My horses were covered by my barn mate, Jann. Jann goes away often.

She tends to join her husband who travels internationally for work and sometimes they stay away for a month or two at a time. During those times I cover her, so now it's my turn. I have a bit of a cushion in the bank. I recently sold my house to move into a small carriage house apartment.

I'd been thinking of selling my house for many years. My son was grown, I was no longer married, I lost my dog several years earlier so there was really no reason to own a three bedroom, 3 1/2 bathroom house any longer. It was purely a sentimental issue. So many times that I thought about selling and simplifying my life, freeing myself from the responsibility of owning a home. I couldn't do it. Then one day a very good friend of mine, Lenore who I knew through the horse world, made a good point to me. I've been so blessed to have amazing friends who have such great perspective! Lenore said to me, over one of our coffee pow-wows, "You can't let go of that house because you think you're going to live forever." I said to her, "I lived my entire adult life there, I raised my son there. I don't know any other home."

Lenore corrected me, "Your home is wherever you make it. The house is just a thing. Things only matter if you're going to live forever, Jessi. Things that are no longer useful to you only hold you back and this house is holding you back."

Lenore was right. A weight was lifted when the offer I would accept came in just six short days after I listed. Another family would now make memories in this house.

Occasionally I drive by on the way to my office and I look fondly on the house, with zero regrets. Ultimately, letting go of the responsibility of owning a home afforded me the financial freedom to make this trek and much more. I'm a hard worker and I never slacked. As a massage therapist I never lit the world on fire with my pay but I was smart with what I had, invested well and that has opened some doors. I still need to be financially judicious but I am comfortable doing a little more and taking a little time off. Jesse was right, I can always make more money but memories have to be made now while I can enjoy them.

I met Cally several years ago and instantly we became friends. Cally and Louise were on a trip together. Louise travels from

Canada and Cally resides outside of Memphis. The duo became friendly through their work. Louise, a stunning blonde bombshell about 46 runs a successful travel agency helping overworked Canadians find refuge in luxurious breaks from reality. Cally, a beautiful fiery redhead in her mid 40's, could have been easily mistaken for a much younger woman. Her career in the Memphis tourism industry is responsible for the professional collaboration with Louise which naturally led to their social alliance. The pair had become very close over their time in the industry, often joking that Cally was the Thelma to her friend Louise.

I sure did luck out when I met these two gorgeous chicas. There I was on the deck of a Carnival Pride cruise ship, soaking in every ounce of the beautiful Caribbean sun on the first five-day trip I had allowed myself in a two-year period. Red Stiletto Boyfriend was in the chaise lounge beside me, seemingly hypnotized by his iPhone, utterly entrenched in whatever internet fantasy rendezvous he was involved in on this particular day. He could not be bothered with sharing any of his attention with me. I was so happy when Cally, or maybe it was Louise, struck up a random conversation over a new brand of sunscreen they noticed me using.

I spent the majority of my time on the ship with these ladies who were destined to remain in my life for many years to come. We were the three musketeers for the remainder of the cruise. By the end of it we were notorious, the mischievous girls who received a lot of turned-up noses from stuffy middle-aged women who secretly wished they could join our ornery brigade but couldn't, for fear of judgment and disapproval from their peers. Once again I was grateful for the simplicity of social media making it effortless to stay in touch with them over the years. Now that I'll be traveling across Tennessee I can visit Cally. Sadly Louise was unable to get away from Canada at this time. "I'm up to my eyeballs in singles cruises and European spa vacations," she regretfully explained. We would be one musketeer short this time.

Rolling up to the grand, monumental entrance of Cally's brand-new sub-division, I glance at the GPS, making sure to stay on course while preparing to explain to security that this truck driving, cowgirl-boot wearing girl really does belong here.

I walk through the door after an agonizing six-hour drive, which should've only been three hours, and my girl had a frozen margarita waiting for me. That is a girl's true friend!

My ride to Olive Branch, Mississippi, was endless but so many jam-ups on the highway gave me a chance to enjoy the CB radio I picked up for this trip. I felt so cool tuning in and listening to the road-weary truckers banter back-and-forth exchanging information and traffic conditions. First I heard one of the truckers, "Well I'll be a monkey's uncle," and then another chimed in, "Now that's what happens when you don't pay attention." I knew it was going to be a long ride at that moment. It took nearly an hour before the crawling traffic gave me a front seat view of the unfortunate jackknifed tractor trailer totally off the shoulder laying on its side halfway into the wooded area several yards from the road.

Now at Cally's, feeling relieved to be where I will stay for the next 24 hours, contentment sweeps through me. There we stood in Cally's kitchen drinking the fruity frozen deliciousness and girl talk picking up right where it had left of several years earlier. Just as I start to feel the stress-diminishing effects of the tequila, Cally informs me we need to rush off to go complete a closing. She's been working part time with a mortgage company and remembered that she had to do a quick closing right now. "What should we do with our drinks," I inquired. "Well duh," she says, "take them with us!".

The suburb of Olive Branch where Cally lives is a brand-new suburb of Memphis. It's in the middle of nowhere, nobody around, yet being a rule follower my whole life this just felt crazy, so I was all in! It is only a few days into this trip and I am already becoming comfortable with the concept of throwing caution to the wind.

We jump into the car, margaritas in the cupholders and head to the closing just five minutes down the road. The truth is it was really the equivalent of having a glass of wine at lunch and then going on with your day but to me a huge jump out of the box of conformity.

The next morning after our coffee, Cally prepared for work. When she was about to leave, she suddenly remembered there was something she wanted to give me. Having worked for the tourism department of the Memphis chamber of commerce, Cally brandished museum tickets for me!

I had no idea what was in store for me while attempting to patronize these museums. Once Cally and I hugged our goodbyes and she left for work I finished my coffee while chatting with her husband and then headed out shortly after her. I quickly entered the address of the first museum into my GPS and pulled out of the circular driveway making my way back to the development gate.

First was the Stax Museum. I pulled my truck into the fenced parking area which was monitored by its own security guard. It was a straight shot from the parking area directly to the entrance of the museum. I spent several hours learning about the fascinating history of soul music and also the history of the museum itself.

I learned the museum celebrates Stax Records which has been around since 1957. Originally known as Satellite Records, it was founded by brother and sister Jim Stewart and Estelle Axton. They combined their names STewart and AXton to come up with the new name, Stax, in 1961. The siblings shared their operations with Volt Records which they formed to avoid showing favoritism. The company was influential in creating the Southern Soul and Memphis Soul style. They also published gospel, funk and blues.

Their biggest star was Otis Redding, "The Big O," also known as the "King of Soul" who tragically died in a plane crash in

1967 at age 26 though not before recording many hits including his first, "These Arms of Mine," in 1962.

Upon entering the museum, the first site I saw was a simulated church adorned with authentic artifacts such as a baptismal bowl and paper church fan. I felt myself transported to his era while immersed in the music and the visuals surrounding me. It was an emotional experience. Blues music was born of hardship and offered African-American slaves relief and release through music. I could literally feel the history.

I wandered through the vinyl-record covered hallways. I learned about many other musical icons. I saw a beautiful, beaded yellow dress that once belonged to Tina Turner and a Telecaster guitar that had once been Ike

Turner's. I saw the contract signed by Sam & Dave for the sale of the song "Soul Man"! If only they had known how big it was going to be I wonder if they would've sold it for $3500 and 50-percent of all royalties over $7000. I saw the blue Cadillac once owned by the creative force Isaac Hayes, with all of its gold details. I found it rather tacky but unquestionably unique. There is a circular dance floor in the middle of the museum, colorful lights swirling and soul music filling the room. I found myself longing for a dance. In that moment I felt a pang of missing Alex, my handsome Roanoke dance partner.

After my mind was full with all of what the Stax had to offer, I got back in my vehicle and headed for Beale Street to see the Museum of Rock and Soul.

Walking along one-way Beale Street, a car slows and the passenger window comes down. The shady-looking character inside gives me a "Hey baby," and keeps mumbling something inaudible. He got louder and I looked over to him. Only for the sake of keeping the peace, I gave a simple smile and nod as I continued along my way. Thankfully, traffic was going the opposite direction that I was walking. I couldn't help but giggle to myself wondering if I would've still gotten the "Hey baby" if he knew I was about to turn fifty.

I continued towards my goal. I could see the small blue and red sign hanging over what I had not yet noticed was a strangely quiet Memphis street. About 30 yards away from the museum, startled by the blaring screech of tires, I jumped to the side thinking that a car was about to crash.

I hear loud angry yelling and quickly lift my eyes to what I now notice is a completely deserted street. The reality of what was happening sent a wave of terror through my veins. Running towards me while threateningly shouting profanities, "You didn't think I'd catch up to you, you didn't think I'd make it back here in time!" was the shady guy from just a few minutes earlier. His car was in the middle of the lane, door wide open, engine running. My heart pounding so hard and fast I could feel it in my throat, I quickly surveyed the area, taking note of the unopened FedEx arena, businesses with no patrons entering or exiting, restaurants with no diners to be seen. How is this possible that noon on a Tuesday, not a holiday, downtown Memphis…Where are all the people? Shouldn't the streets be full of tourists and people who work in the city going to lunch? There was not a soul in sight, no cars driving down the street. In the seconds it took me to form these thoughts my would-be attacker, possibly kidnapper, was closing the distance between us and I had no plan. Suddenly the reality set in that this could be where my vacation ends, it could be where everything ends. I prepared to fight.

I know what they say, when you think you might die your life flashes before your eyes. This did not occur. I know when there is an attack they say it all happened so fast. It was not fast at all. Time moved as if in a slow-motion NFL replay video.

As if in some low-budget, predictable movie, a couple rounded the corner just in the nick of time. I sprinted to them uncertain if they would be willing to help. I told them I didn't know this man that was following me and he was scaring me.

They told me to stand there with them. The man told me to pretend I was with them and keep talking to them even as the furious guy continued to scream profanities and make lunges towards us. Every time he would lurch forward, the man from the couple would look up and the shady man would back off. Finally, he got back in his car and left. Feeling relieved I thanked the duo and they walked off to find lunch. I made a fast dash for the museum door because I knew I would be safe inside there and I would be able to find somebody to walk me back to my truck.

As I grabbed the door handle and pull, it wouldn't move. I looked up and my heart sank, the sign on the door read, "Closed On Tuesdays." I did make it safely back to my truck and happily put Memphis in my rear-view mirror, now on Interstate 40 traveling in the direction of Colorado. The gravity of the danger I just faced had not yet settled in, though I knew I would be much more careful moving forward.

In the time I was preparing for this trip, whenever I shared my plans with people, most would react with shock and tell me how brave I am to travel the country alone. I could not understand this because it is America after all. My close friends who knew me well were not concerned or surprised by my ambitions. I didn't think it was that big of a deal. I figured people travel short distances all the time and this was in effect simply a compilation of many short trips. Regardless, I do take a shine to thinking of myself in a high percentile of badasses. I would find that station challenged many times over the next few weeks.

Chapter 6

You Can't Make This Stuff Up

The moment that the full impact of the previous event started to hit me, things abruptly escalated to excitement again. If what was currently unfolding, just thirty short minutes after hightailing it out of Memphis had been a scene in a movie, I would have been convinced the director had completely jumped the shark. Before leaving for this trip, I had hoped for adventure, this was not exactly what I had in mind.

As the parade of high speed, siren-screaming police cars zoomed past me on Interstate 40 in Arkansas, like a herd of expeditiously stampeding antelope, I was

back to the highway I felt a pang of anxiety. Things continue to fall in place, in the not too far distance I see a DOT vehicle. The kind man informed me that if I continued on 261 until I hit 70 that would take me ten miles ahead and I can jump back on 40.

Turning onto 70 I realize I need a break. Fatigued, hungry and suddenly slightly suspicious of new surroundings, I'm reluctant to stop but an opportunity presents. A broken-down milk truck sat at the edge of a gravel parking lot with an American flag flying proudly off a telephone pole. The vintage 1960's Ford classic, still rusty, had been creatively painted with distressed blue and flowers of red and white. A gold background behind the name of the business, under the flowers and surrounded by the blue, created the cutest bumpkinly sign. The country diner was nothing more than a large metal pole barn-type building sitting lonely in the center of the lot with a few cars parked outside. Getting closer to the building door revealed another American flag and a sign that for some reason made me instantly comfortable, "Female Owned Business." Although I could not see inside through the tinted-glass door and absence of windows, I confidently yet cautiously opened the door. To my surprise, joy and relief this place was amazing! It was pure country rustic beauty! The walls were a delightful mixture of wooden uppers with a patina tin roof from chair-height down. Handmade eyelet lace curtains and floral arrangements complimented the many adorable sentimental decorations, clearly chosen with care giving the restaurant a homey, personal feeling. The clever country décor filled my soul and the delicious, fresh smalltown meal cured my hunger. The conversation with the few locals that were inside would fill me up even more.

I was finally at ease when a neighbor in obvious distress burst through the door and advised us to lockdown because a man with a rifle is loose in the area and he had just shot a cop in the arm and stolen his squad car.

Standing up a little straighter while sweeping a wisp of runaway hair from in front of her eye, the restaurant owner in true country-girl style responded with a definitive, "I am not locking my door!" She proclaimed this with such certainty that I knew it would be a bad day for that fugitive if he dared set foot in her building. I am pretty sure that the blonde haired, blue-eyed, little Southern belle had a 12-gauge shotgun and a strong set of brass lady nuts behind the counter which was adorned with the sign reading, "Eat Here. It's Homemade."

I always admire how these well-groomed, polite, sweet country women can instantly turn on their strong, battle-ready attitude like the flick of a light switch. I knew I was safer here with her than anywhere, but my instincts told me it was a sign to get back to my travels. It was a bit of a downer to say goodbye to the friendly Arkansas crew, though I am sure I will return one day.

Back in my truck, before continuing down CR-70, I quickly posted a brief blog entry on social media about this experience. More about the amazing little hidden gem of a diner than anything else so I was flabbergasted when I received a phone call from a local TV reporter requesting an interview. I explained that I didn't see much more than a police chase and he rebutted, "Well, that's more than I have now," so I obliged. I pulled over in the shoulder and did the Zoom interview with the reporter. After watching myself later on the Palestine, Arkansas evening news, I learned that the very dangerous criminal had crossed several states committing several violent crimes. He had now barricaded himself in a home about one mile from the diner. Nothing ever happens in the quiet rural town however, the police might not be practiced but they were skilled and managed to quell the situation and capture the suspect and no one else got hurt. I was also glad to learn that the officer injured would recover just fine.

I was finally able to make my way back to Interstate 40 to continue through Arkansas. I traveled for a bit when I heard the CB which had been quiet for some time. "Put some gas to that Chevy would ya!," joked the trucker that shot past me at about 90 miles an hour. We wound up chatting on CB for the next 30 minutes. He was a fun and interesting distraction from all the crazy of this day. He was quite the character, "What do you do in your off time?" I asked. "I like whiskey and sinning," was his response, and that seemed about right for this rugged Southern old guy just out here loving the road and making a living. I said goodbye to my fiery, ornery road companion when I found the need to pull off and find a ladies room.

Remembering how rural this area was I was not surprised when I couldn't find one. After a few minutes of driving around looking for an option to solve the problem, I luckily found a construction site on a back road and it had a Porta-potty. Not ideal but seemed par for the course on this trip.

Missing the quiet of the country road where the diner had been I decided to try and make a break from the interstate and take the road less traveled once again. I jumped off at the next exit but quickly navigated back to 40 as I got nervous about being alone and no idea where I was. Time for an encouraging phone call. I got on the phone first with Lucy in Colorado and then with Brittany in Florida, these two know me utterly well. Both ladies shared the opinion of "You can do this," and "You didn't set out on this journey to look at the interstate, you want to see the real America." They were right, I needed to cowgirl-up and do what I was here to do. Pushing down the discomfort and anxiety took a gargantuan willfulness.

Now getting closer to the Oklahoma state line I started toying with jumping on and off of the interstate, building my bravery with more exits between each return until I was so far from the interstate that the GPS wouldn't bring me back to it. What I had failed to understand about this great country of ours is how entirely uninhabited most of it is. Finding fuel, food and lodging was proving to be a substantial problem in these parts. As it got later in the day I had resigned to the fact that I might be spending another night in my truck but this time in a much more unpopulated area and again felt apprehension.

Ahead there is an entrance to what seems like a bigger road. It is CR-64 and with cow fields my only backdrop, I enter. It is a bigger road but still no people and only the occasional stray vehicle passing in the opposite direction. After a little while I notice my fuel is at about half so I tell Siri to navigate to the nearest gas station. To my horror it doesn't work. A fast glance at my iPhone screen tells me I have a virus in my phone. I'm in the middle of nowhere and after a moment of pure panic I pull myself together and start looking for the next exit and after several miles I see one. It appears nothing but farmland there but I pull off anyway to see if I can reach Apple to fix my phone. Another blessing in disguise! What I couldn't see from the highway was the Cherokee Casino & Hotel. I thought, Jackpot! apologizing to myself for the bad pun.

What started out as what seemed to be an unfortunate incident with my phone turned into the most comfortable option for the night. Even better, when I got in contact with Apple they determined it to be a phishing attempt and not a virus, easily removed in the settings. Thank God it happened when it did because this was not only the last decent hotel for many miles, it was the only hotel for many miles.

The light turned green as I held the key card up to the door and I entered the modern room. I got a shower, primped a little and took the elevator back downstairs to find dinner and entertainment. It was a new hotel and I guess still largely unknown as there were not many people around and all but the cafeteria-style restaurant was closed. I didn't care, I was able to get a meal. I had a conversation with another guest while I ate and when I was done eating, I played a few slots. I didn't win.

Morning came and I took full advantage of the creature comforts the hotel had to offer. I got a quick workout in the extremely limited fitness center, enjoyed the included breakfast and a glorious hot shower.

In preparation for the impending journey, I carefully picked out my most comfortable jeans, knowing the only guarantee for today would be many long hours in the driver's seat. I stuffed the last few pieces of clothing into my bag, threw it over my shoulder and made my way out of the hotel room to the lobby. After thanking the people at the casino hotel desk, I sauntered through the parking lot to my truck, tossed my bag onto the backseat, hopped in and buckled up. My plan was to make it to Lucy's in Pueblo, Colorado, by tomorrow evening.

Chapter 7

Pumpjacks and Wind Turbines

The time we spend in solitude brings about a unique kind of transformational growth that does not occur when we're surrounded by the stimulation, verbal communication, visual and audio entertainment, and the daily rituals and commitments that we all face.

A different kind of listening takes over when all of the noise has ceased, when all of the clamor of daily expectations are put aside and replaced with basic, primal needs.

The life-changing breath inhaled from behind the wheel on a desolate country road is a different kind of oxygen. It fuels and motivates those who are energized by adventure, new sights and sounds, and new experiences. My heart is full in these moments.

Having grown up in the suburbs of Philadelphia, before today I believed that Lancaster, Pennsylvania, with its Amish communities and endless farms was rural. I had no idea what rural actually was. In fact traveling through Oklahoma was not simply rural, it was completely void of civilization altogether. I am quickly learning that much of the United States is incredibly uninhabited.

When making the decision to leave the interstate behind and take the secondary road spanning east to west across the Oklahoma panhandle, I had no idea how utterly alone I would find myself. There were times I could go as far as 100 miles without seeing anything. Not a farm, a gas station or even a crossroad.

My only companions were the road, the occasional oil pumpjack, and thousands of wind turbines lining the horizon as far as the eye could see, stretching all the way into oblivion. It was easy to daydream of a world long after the extinction of mankind. I imagined myself in a post-apocalyptic time, an age in which humanity had vanished from the Earth, leaving behind only this mysterious army of steadfast wind turbine soldiers. Ominous. Imposing. Stretching upward into a dark blanket of low hanging clouds. Winds in a constant state of motion across the prairies of Oklahoma as though some extramundane fan had been placed at the state line and the air flow from it emanating into eternity.

How can the clouds be so still while the wind continues to blow?

Many hours behind the wheel transmuted Oklahoma Route 270 into the Ghosts of Jessie's Life Past, Present and Future. My mind had the luxury of wandering through memories, examining the present and exploring the future.

There was a period of time in my younger years that I could not figure out the reason I existed. I gave this more thought than the average young adult might. I gave it a tremendous amount of power, it ate at me, consumed me. Then one random day, while driving in my little red GEO Prism, I stopped at a red light and I had an epiphany. I was just twenty years of age and eight months pregnant. The light turned green, I shifted my foot from the brake to the gas and in that exact moment I knew. I was here to raise this child. That was my purpose and I never questioned it again, not until I was 48 and my boy was a grown man.

When setting out on this odyssey somehow I knew I would find my new purpose. I think deep down I knew that was the reason I planned this expedition in the first place, not just to have experiences but to realize my place in the world.

So much time, so many concepts, memories and situations to reflect on during this drive. On this deserted road in Oklahoma, I took all of the restrictions off my mind and released it to go where it would go. I let all the barriers down and did nothing to hold my thoughts back.

I first started thinking about the three biggest heartbreaks of my earlier years. Wes was the first. My first true love. Wes owned a tow truck company in Philadelphia. He did what was known as wreck chasing. So many nights I went with him we sat listening to the police scanners under the roadway where Interstate 95 met 676. We would listen, waiting to hear news of an accident and then when an incident was reported we would drive really, really fast, trying to be the first ones there and hopefully win the job. The first truck on the scene usually got the tow job and that meant also that they would bring the damaged vehicle to the body shop they are affiliated with and get a percentage of the repair job.

Wes and I had fun every time we got together. Even if we were just wreck chasing. We had fun when we went out, we had fun when we went dancing, we had fun when we went to hear jazz music. We had fun staying in and watching movies together and talking and laughing. It seemed like the perfect relationship, except... He told me what he wanted, or more importantly what he did not want.

One thing that it would take me several more broken hearts to learn is that when somebody tells you who they are and when somebody tells you what they want, you need to believe them. When they tell you what they're willing to give, you need to believe them. So many young girls make the same mistake I did when I got together with Wes in my early 20s. We believe that we can love a man so much that it will make him love us back, even when they tell us they don't want anything serious. His words would say he didn't want anything serious but his actions told me so much more, I thought. Actions speak louder than words, right? I would learn, well yes, except when he is being clear and telling you he is not interested in a relationship.

Wes and I did everything together over the almost two years we were together. We would see each other several times throughout the week. We had exciting and fun evenings out dancing and listening to our favorite bands. Wes would tell me it was nothing serious but yet I knew I was the only girl in his life and he was certainly the only guy in

mine. I believed telling me nothing serious
was just something that he said, not
something that he actually meant. When we
made love, it was wildly passionate and I was
so sure we were deeply connected. I imagined
the way he would look at me after meant
more, confirming in my mind that he was my
forever guy. That is, until the day that I
learned he wasn't. I was driving down
Columbus Boulevard and I saw his tow truck
parked outside of Hooters, surely waiting for
the scanners to reveal the next chase
opportunity. I was so excited at my good
fortune for running into him unexpectedly
and getting an extra unplanned visit. He'll be
so happy to see me. I had a couple of
girlfriends in the car with me and I said, "I'm
just going to pull over and say hi to Wes real
quick." Running up to the driver-side

window, I knocked on it. He wasn't opening the door or the window, strange. Then I knocked on it harder because I could see there was definitely someone in there. I could vaguely make out the silhouette of a person in the driver's seat through the tinted window. It crossed my mind that maybe somebody else was using his truck and was wondering who this girl knocking on the window is. Then I saw another silhouette appear as she sat up. He opened the door. It took a minute for me to process what I had just witnessed between the Hooters girl and Wes and for that information to register in my mind.

It took me nearly a year to recover.

The second lost love was several years later. This story would put the writers of Lifetime Network movies to shame. He was the wolf in sheep's clothing. Skillfully able to manipulate almost any situation by playing on the inherent nurturing nature of a woman. The pain endured when the betrayal was revealed seemed as though it would sear through every ounce of me for the rest of my existence. It didn't, though I still had not fully learned.

Five years after that, there was Red Stiletto Guy. This was where the most consequential and extraordinary of my growth happened. It was over the nearly thirteen years that I imprisoned myself in this one-sided, often cruel, and always unfulfilling relationship that I began my journey into becoming a stronger and more confident woman. I learned to heal the injured, insecure girl and move on from her, leaving her in my wake. I have made a conscious effort toward this and became an active participant in molding myself into the woman that I can honestly like and truly respect. I won't say this is easy. It takes hard work, willingness to see the parts of oneself that are not pleasant to see and the blessing of awareness. It took a great effort not to allow these experiences to leave any negative marks on me. I thank God that I was able to benefit from them, use them as fertilizer for the growth ahead and continue to flourish each day since that shift happened in my soul.

I once had a knack for choosing emotionally unavailable men with broken empathy. Now I recognize these men quickly and avoid them.

Flash forward and shortly after I return home from this current trip, my growth will be tested, I will meet a man who almost steals my heart. The lessons from the past will save me. The enlightenment gained, partially from this journey, will save me. I will walk away from him when I am not ready to, because I will know I have to, he is not able to give what I require.

For the first time in my life I would be able to walk away from something that I still wanted. I would make the choice because of the truth that he told me. It will take me two weeks from the time that he makes his confession and every ounce of strength that I had banked over the years to do it. The pain, as intense as I expected, until the time that it subsides. Afterwards I was that much stronger.

With each heartbreak comes new progression and an opportunity to increase emotional intelligence and gain new levels of strength. I thought about what a huge gift it is to get such profound take-aways from what would otherwise be pointless pain. On the long, straight, windy, lonely stretch of Route 270 these memories lead me into my next daydream and topic of thought.

Chapter 8

Definitions and Discoveries

"You're brave," became the predictable response no matter who I shared my upcoming travel plans with. "You're brave." What I thought to be such an odd reaction seemed to be extremely common.

I am planning a road trip. An exhilarating, fun, honky-tonk to honky-tonk, dance from state to state, National Park visiting, small-town America discovering, U.S.A. exploration adventure.

Brave?

Words are easy to say without much thought, after all it is how we communicate. We tend to dangerously overuse words, which when presented properly, connote powerful meaning. This current trend creates disconnect and diminishes the importance of the historical context of certain words, terms and their definitions so the language inadvertently becomes substantially less impactful.

The number of people who declared me brave in this situation sparked my curiosity and the long stretch on Oklahoma 270 gave me time to think about it. What is bravery after all? I was inspired to explore the differences and connections between bravery, strength and independence, the definition and the varying interpretations of each. Most importantly, if any of these qualities can exist in the absence of the others.

What the dictionary will tell us about each of these words is this.

Definition of brave: Having or showing mental or moral strength to face moral or physical danger, fear, or difficulties

Definition of strength: Power to resist force SOLIDITY, TOUGHNESS

Not easily broken or torn

Definition of independent: Not subject to control by others, not affiliated with a larger controlling unit, not requiring or relying on something else not contingent, not looking to others for one's opinions or for guidance in conduct, not requiring or relying on others, showing a desire for freedom.

Although this next definition is technically intended to describe mathematical equations, it is the one I relate to the most. I read it entirely differently than Mr. Webster intended. It goes like this:

"not determined by or capable of being deduced or derived from or expressed in terms of members (such as axioms or equations) of the set under consideration." Dictionary definitions aside, there is so much more to discover about these qualities.

I continue on the long straight unending highway. Temporarily snapped out of my state of deep thought by the occasional semi-truck whizzing by in the opposite direction. Thankfully, the satellite radio is still picking up Y2Kountry, although the cell signal is spotty at best. Sinking back into my own head after the last truck distraction, my mind picked up where it left off.

Perhaps Bravery should be defined as understanding the risk and still going forward without concern to take on a challenge. It is believing you can accomplish whatever you're facing but still knowing there is a possibility you won't succeed and pressing forward regardless because the end result is worth it.

Can you use bravery to describe somebody taking a fun jaunt across the country and also use the same word for a soldier running towards gunfire into battle? Can you use it for somebody who is afraid of heights and goes over the Raton Pass or for somebody who has suffered through social anxiety going out of the house on their own for the first time in years?

The answer is undoubtedly yes. Bravery doesn't have to meet a certain risk threshold because it's not a level playing field. It is a situational sliding scale dependent on a person's tolerance. When people look at someone else's action as brave, the person doing the action usually doesn't see themself that way. The observer sees an action as brave because it is something that scares them, so they project the bravery it would take for themself onto the person doing the action. Others might use the word brave to describe something in someone else, when to that person bravery has nothing to do with it, it's just something that they do without a second thought. In addition, things that you would think should take bravery sometimes don't and things that seem much safer and easier sometimes take the most bravery as each person owns their own internal sliding scale. To some, going out on a dance floor in public may be scarier and require more bravery than running into the gunfire of war. Comfort levels and fear levels are not necessarily progressive, it really is random inside of each person.

Before delving far into it, I would've thought that strength and bravery could be synonymous. Through curiosity and conversation I've learned that the truth is that there are distinct differences between these two qualities. The largest difference being that strength is gained by resistance and adaptation to adversity, whereas bravery being an inherent ability to face challenge, risk and danger regardless of outcome.

My friends often tell me, "Jessi, you are one of the strongest women I know." I don't know why they see me that way. I hear it all the time. As I ponder the women in my history that I view as intensely strong, I never regarded myself in that circle.

A plethora of questions dance around my mind. Is maintaining a composed exterior in moments of weakness a display of strength? If you are a truly strong person, can you have episodes of weakness? I think people often confuse strength with independence. I'm definitely independent. No doubt.

Some people think it's strong that I like to take myself out for an evening to places where I don't know anyone. Again independence. Some people think it's strong that I raised a child alone at a very young age. That is not strength, that is simply dealing with the situation that you find yourself in and in this case a pleasure and a blessing, a privilege.

Some people tell me that I am strong because I finally walked away from the unsatisfying relationship with Red Stiletto Guy. I don't see strength there. I did everything I could to fix it. I sought information on how to communicate, how to be a good partner but most of all how to be a person I would want to be with. That's not strength, it's an understanding that I had a lot to learn, the ability to accept that fact and the bandwidth to seek out the knowledge. That's not strength, that's also a gift. I stayed in that situation until the lesson was learned, then I removed myself from it. That wasn't strength, that was simply knowing when to walk away. It was easy.

Some people tell me I'm strong for building my own business, for choosing my own path rather than going into the family business. I don't see that as strength, I see that as not wanting to live somebody else's dream. I see that as wanting my own accomplishments and to discover my own worth, not wanting anything I didn't earn. I see that once again as independence. I think that independence is a much more tangible concept than strength. I can easily define it. Strength is a more abstract and idealistic notion.

A huge gust of forceful Oklahoma wind slammed into the Chevy nearly throwing me off the road and again ripping me away from thoughts of these engaging questions. Heart pounding, I take a deep breath, a sip of water and a quick peek at the fuel gauge. Slightly below half, not a great thing in this part of the country with sometimes a hundred miles between gas stations. I was grateful that the GPS was working and I could see there would be fuel in about 60 miles. I slipped back into my thoughts.

So, what is Strength? Perhaps strength is the condition of being stoic. Having a composed demeanor and staying emotionally level in any situation and never losing your cool. Perhaps a strong person is someone that people trust and who creates a feeling of confidence in others just by being in their presence. Maybe what separates strength from bravery is that strength requires some sort of struggle. Such as the bodybuilder that knows that building muscle strength requires resistance. Somebody may have a predisposition to being strong but they won't know that until they have faced adversity and that it's been tested. Strength requires conflict. It is an acquired and learned quality of which struggle is a large component.

The next part is, what exactly is Independence? Typically an independent person has their shit together. They don't need other people around to make them feel happy or successful or wanted. These people are fully comfortable on their own, but they also find value in spending time with others. An independent person makes careful choices on who they're willing to share their time with because they understand that time is precious. The opinions of others do not define independent people. They are not lonely when they're alone, they enjoy their own company and are wholly comfortable in their personal space. These people are defined by their own path, their own goals and accomplishments. "They run their own race."

What I didn't yet know was that throughout the six weeks to come all three of these qualities would be tested, observed and realized within me.

The flat prairie lands of the Oklahoma panhandle stretched on and on, the reed-like grasses displaying the strength of the wind. After many hours of driving, the tiny gas station and country store against the backdrop of the brilliant pink dusk sky was a welcome relief. Although I hadn't seen any people and only the occasional semi-truck for hours, I did see a sign promising a town 80 miles ahead.

The gas station sat out of place and lonely on the northeast corner of a deserted crossroads. In the other three directions only endless pristine prairie land. I jumped out of the truck, fighting to hold my hair out of my face against the relentless Oklahoma winds and made my way to the first sign of salvation in over 100 miles. Inside the tiny, modest store there was one other customer bustling around, looking at an item here and there without much interest. Behind the counter sat a friendly, sixtyish woman sporadically exchanging bits of mundane conversation with the customer.

After her warm country welcome I told her I was traveling to Pueblo, Colorado, and that I saw the sign for a town ahead. I explained in my obviously suburban way that I wanted to get as close to Pueblo as possible and if I made it to the town on the sign, how far was it to the next one. The idyllic outland woman was amused by my naivety to the actual vastness of the Midwest. It was hard to absorb, being there was nothing in my former life to equate it to.

She told me that Guymon, the next town, was the last town until I reached Pueblo. I asked her about hotels off the highway and she said, "Nope, none of that either until Pueblo. You better just stay in Guymon for the night, it's going to be dark soon." So I decided to look for a hotel room in Guymon.

When driving in the Midwest it's not like in the East where cities slowly make way for the suburbs and as you continue further from the cities the suburbs slowly thin out into country and then farmland. In the Midwest and West you can drive through nothingness for hours. You could drive and drive and drive and see nothing at all and then boom, just like that you're in a town. There is no gradual appearance of a house and then another house and then a couple more houses progressively becoming denser like in the East. Out here there's nothing and then suddenly you're in a town, when you go out the other side of the town there's immediately nothing again.

When I reached Guymon I had my choice of four hotels so I stayed at a Holiday Inn which was the best the town offered. I looked for someplace to grab a bite and maybe find some entertainment. I found a decent sized pub which was definitely the nicest and most modern restaurant in town. I walked in and the local people seemed great. What a happy crowd. I walked up to the bar and grabbed an empty chair next to a few jolly men, probably in their mid sixties. Everyone was friendly and welcoming. The man directly next to me was a good-natured widower who shared the chronicle of his past with me. I think he was appreciative of a fresh face and a listening ear. I appreciated him trusting me with his story. After dinner I tried what was suggested as a fun little country bar which turned out to be just a little bar, no music and no atmosphere. I wound up going back to the hotel and going to sleep early.

The next morning after fueling up I pulled the Chevy back onto the secondary

Oklahoma thruway and headed west. To get to Colorado from Oklahoma you have to go through a small corner of New Mexico. The New Mexico landscape is majestic and unique, I'd never seen anything like it. While lost in admiring the mesmerizing mesas in the distance, behind a herd of antelope grazing carefree and untroubled on a meal of desert brush, I dodged a rattlesnake coiled up in the street. Just before reaching the state line, I stopped again for fuel in a small commercial area clearly designed to accommodate weary travelers. It has been several hours since I left Guymon, making only one other stop when I happened upon a brown sign which I recognized as an historic marker. I had taken a moment to stop in the narrow pull-off overlooking the Sierra Grande, the largest extinct volcano in New Mexico.

At the gas station while fueling up I didn't understand why I was suddenly feeling funny, my head had become frighteningly foggy. I had to work hard to manifest thoughts. "You don't look so good," I heard coming from the adjacent pump. There was no one else nearby so it was surely meant for me. "Well thanks a whole hell of a lot, mister," I joked back. The man, who I learned was traveling the opposite direction, told me what I was feeling was altitude sickness. I was at almost 6700 feet. He instructed me to drink a lot of water and take a few minutes to rest. Once I gathered myself enough to drive safely I continued along my way. Soon I would find myself challenged by the intimidating Raton Pass.

Chapter 9

Adventures with Lucy

Safely at Lucy's, after dinner and good conversation, still feeling quite shaken from the Raton Pass experience, it was time for a steam bath and a good night sleep. Funny how the mountain pass left me much more traumatized than the events in Memphis had. I tried to release some of that anxiety while sitting on the warm towel Lucy had set out for me on the tile bench in the shower stall. Turning on the steam dial the glass enclosure started to fill with soothing, balmy mist. I watched condensation beads form on the large coral colored tiles covering the walls while imagining myself in a tropical rainforest amongst the beautiful collection of green plants lined up on the oversize vanity and window sills. Lucy had left me the most calming lavender castile soap and a lovely bottle of vitamin D oil to combat the dry Colorado air. After my steam shower I rinsed with cooler water and dried off, feeling quite restored. I climbed into a snug, cushy bed with king-size pillows and fluffy down comforter. I slept soundly.

After a fresh breakfast consisting of all items from her parents' gardens in Rye, Lucy and I spent the day in Rye, Colorado, hiking to an amazing natural arch in San Isabel National Forest. After completing the vigorous hike that took us all the way to 7,000 feet in elevation, we rewarded ourselves with a fun stop on the way home and took a detour to visit Bishop Castle. The castle is an incredible and interesting landmark. It is an eerie-looking structure with rickety catwalks of hand-curled ironwork high above its base. Every board, brick and curl in the ironwork built by the hand of Jim Bishop. At 15 years old Jim Bishop had saved 452 dollars and bought two and a half acres of land surrounded on three sides by San Isabel National Forest in southern Colorado. He did anything he could: He mowed lawns, he delivered newspapers and he worked in his fathers business which was ornamental iron working. Young Jim Bishop's parents agreed to sign for the land for him because at 15 he was not allowed to legally make the purchase. Jim and his father spent many years camping and enjoying the land with the idea that Jim would build a cabin on the property. As he worked on the cabin, problems would come up and he would solve them. He built a little at a time. Many of his friends and family joked that it looked like he was building a castle. He liked that idea. One day when somebody once again joked, "What are you building? A castle?" Jim responded with, "Yes, I am going to be building a castle," and the dream was born. Jim worked for sixty years building the castle and he's still not done. It's a constant living, breathing creature in its own right. Now hosting a fire breathing dragon, a grand ballroom, three full stories of stonework with towers and iron bridges twisting between them, the peculiar, grandiose oddity stands overlooking the San Isabel forest.

At the time I didn't know that it was a big deal but the eccentric Jim Bishop himself got out of his truck and did a little dance with me. I saw the man sitting in his truck, apparently he is normally not at all social, but I didn't know that when I made my comment, "So there's the man behind the magic!" Jim quickly snapped back with a riposte, "I don't know why everyone is so excited about all this over here! Don't they know I can dance?" Well, this was fantastic I thought. "What kind of dance do you do?" was my inquiry.

"I used to swing dance with my wife when she was living, I am a great dancer!" I asked if he would honor me with a dance and all 5'3" of this eccentric older gentleman hopped out of his truck. He took my hands and spun me starting the first of two dances. As tourists stood around watching this phenomenon and cheering from time to time, Jim commented on there being no music.

There was no cellular or wifi signal at the site, so playing tracks was not an option.

"No worries sir, the music is in my head and I can tell you are playing the same song in your mind that I am." I thanked him for the dance and Lucy and I returned to her truck.

I spent the next forty-eight hours with Lucy exploring the town of Pueblo and realizing that it really is a great little town despite its poor reputation. We visited the riverwalk and had a fantastic dinner. We found a cute little country bar and did a couple of line dances. We spent wonderful girl time talking while sinking into her oversized leather couch, cozying up with fleece blankets in the shadow of the beautiful Colorado sunset which poured in through the glass wall facing the mountains.

We visited her parents' little homestead where they grew tiny patches of every vegetable you can think of. We picked fresh kale and asparagus, then gathered fresh eggs as a small flock of chickens pecked at the ground hunting for tasty morsels of seeds and insects all around us.

Later that evening I enjoyed a steam bath in Lucy's spa-like guest bathroom. I snuggled into my jammies and met her downstairs for a glass of wine and one last girl talk session. I would really miss her until the next time. In the interim we will do our regular FaceTime powwows to get us through.

As my time with Lucy was nearing its end, I mentally prepared myself for the LaVeta Pass. It took everything I had in me to find the bravery needed to head toward the mountain pass. I knew it would be terrifying for me, however seeing Christine was the outcome that was worth the risk and the challenge. I was determined to see my childhood friend after more than a thirty-year hiatus.

I spent a full day and a half with Christine and her husband, Ron. They live on their forty-acre farm in a modest house trailer. The couple makes up for what they lacked in finances with such an abundance of love! When I first arrived and saw Christine for the first time in thirty years it felt like we hadn't skipped a beat. I was so impressed with their family. When Christine took me inside her house so that I could get a drink of water, she looked out the window at her husband of twenty years, turned to me and said, "Isn't he the most handsome man you've ever seen?"

Their love for each other and the love between their entire family, children and grandchildren, was eye-opening and breathtaking. I watched Christine work with her husband on the farm and they were like a well-oiled machine barely needing to say a word to one another because their nonverbal communication was extraordinary. The connection between them was rare and fantastic. I enjoyed seeing my friend so happy. She spent a lot of her youth struggling. Her father left this planet far too soon and her mother could not hold it together for her kids. Seeing her with Ron, all of the suffering of the past was unquestionably put to rest. Christine and Ron were so welcoming and I enjoyed an overnight stay in their RV where they loaned me their dog to cuddle with me. The dog was the perfect protection and company.

We enjoyed another few hours of our reunion in the morning over Christine's home cooked breakfast. They offered to drive me across the La Veta Pass; Christine would drive my truck and Ron would follow to take her home. On the way to visit them the mountain was on my side of the road and the drop off was on the side of oncoming traffic. I really didn't think I could make it back across the pass. Not only was the drop-off on my side, there were breaks in the guardrail for where the highway department would push snow off the road in the winter. I couldn't imagine who would want that job. Plowing snow on a mountain pass and pushing it over the ledge of a thousand-foot drop. I wondered what kind of adrenaline-junkie would be the one to take that job. Anyway, I was in a mindset to push myself into exposure therapy so I graciously declined this assistance and I asked them if there was another way that wasn't quite as intimidating.

Thinking back to the way the Raton pass threw me, I was starting to feel slightly defeated and questioned my own bravery and abilities. I had to snap myself out of that and taking the easy way out would not be productive. I shared this fleeting emotion with my girlfriend Mandy back at home. I didn't know this, but Mandy shared the same fear of heights. She had done extensive research on it and to my dismay it turns out that it is genetic.

Mandy said, "I promise you, you did not lose your badass status! This one is in your genes." She sent me an article which informed me that there are apparently 392 genetic markers associated with this fear. Acrophobia is actually hardwired in some people as part of the evolutionary fight and flight response associated with survival. Most don't even know they have this issue until their first exposure. It usually comes as a surprise to them and the only cure seems to be exposure therapy.

In that moment I made it a point that I would push myself as hard as I could without it becoming dangerous. I had made this trip a mission for self-improvement and I refused to fail.

Christine and Ron told me that I would probably be fine heading back to Route 25 via Bighorn Canyon and going over 8 Mile Hill into Cañon City. "The mountain will be on your side and the drop off on the opposite side. The only place where you might be a little uncomfortable is when you go over 8 Mile Hill," explained Ron. Christine added, "It's not bad." My response to Christine was, "I know what 'not bad' means to you people out here!" I gave her a nervous giggle. She responded with a snarky, "Flatlander."

So, the decision was made. I would take my chances against the 8 Mile Hill. I will say it was challenging although the canyon was absolutely beautiful. I left their house by way of the Poncha Pass which really is not bad and then entered Bighorn Canyon outside of

Salida. I was inside the canyon driving along the river, once again admiring the beauty of our incredible country. Most of this drive to Cañon City was easy for me and some of it made me uncomfortable, but not so uncomfortable that I couldn't do it now after all of the practice I have had the last couple of weeks. The only time I had a visceral reaction to the height was in the very last moment going over the summit of 8 Mile Hill. In that one moment, all of the land disappeared from either side of me and I felt as though my truck was flying in the clouds. By the time my stomach dropped out and my head started to spin I was already over the summit and in Cañon City, a sign for 8-Mile Bar and Grill off to my left. I thought about stopping for a drink and random conversation but decided to keep going instead. The feeling was an immense sense of accomplishment. I was one step closer to beating this phobia.

Chapter 10

America the Beautiful

I was feeling both satisfied and pensive after my visits with Lucy and Christine, knowing that it would be quite some time before I would see them again. I made my way north on Highway 25.

I traveled through Colorado Springs and saw a billboard off the highway advertising the Rodeo Hall of Fame. Spontaneity can become addictive. Unplanned experiences are almost more attractive than the planned ones. How cool to see a sign and decide, I think I will do this today. After a quick unexpected stop and tour of this unique museum, I was back on the road heading towards Wyoming. I decided to spend the night in Casper. It was starting to get late and I didn't want to drive for too long after dark.

Anxiety was growing in me in anticipation of the next day's travel as I was now realizing that the trauma of the Raton Pass was still very much with me and bigger than I had thought. As much as I wanted to push myself out of my comfort zone, as I had on the La Veta Pass and 8 Mile Hill, I realized I had to take some smaller steps depending on my bravery capacity each day. Recognizing this, I stopped at a gas station and after filling up I spoke to the attendant. She was genuinely kind and took her time to open up a map and work with me on finding a route to Yellowstone Park via Montana, through Bozeman and Livingston that did not involve any frightening mountain passes. She assured me that if I went in the west entrance of Yellowstone that it would be fairly mild, and warned me just don't attempt the ride to the grand Tetons from there because you won't like the scenery. I was grateful and thanked her profusely then set out to explore my current surroundings. I found a nice local pub and enjoyed dinner at the bar finding myself in conversation with another random traveler.

The next morning I began my drive to Montana and Yellowstone National Park. Looking for dancing all along the way I decided to stop in Billings hoping to find a honky-tonk. I did find some things online that looked promising but after pulling off the highway and remembering the Memphis experience I quickly decided Billings was not the town for me. Perhaps I simply got off in a tougher neighborhood, maybe a different exit would be a more desirable section of the city but I figured it wasn't worth the risk.

I got back on the highway and made my way to Livingston. It's a small Montana town that one of my massage clients told me about. Livingston is her hometown, she is expressly proud of it and plans to move back when the right work opportunity presents. She said, "In lieu of Jackson Hole go to Livingston, you won't regret it."

Happy that I took her advice, I absolutely fell in love with this tiny, picturesque, nostalgic mountain town, set in a decade long past. I stayed at the Murray Hotel which was an experience in itself, the lobby filled with taxidermy animals, a piano, 1920's decor and a period-preserved elevator that has to be operated by the hotel staff. It's a charmingly historic, family owned business. I took the original brass keys that the young clerk handed me and followed her to the antique elevator in which she took me up to my room. She opened the brass cage and I entered after her. She closed it behind us and held down the button for the third floor.

The room had plenty of modern amenities but still had a feeling that inspired me to watch Turner Classic Movies on the TV.

I explored the town that evening and found a great little restaurant with friendly patrons to socialize with though the town shut down early and by 10 o'clock I was back in my room. I was sad to leave the next day, I absolutely could've stayed longer but I knew I had to continue if I wanted to make it to Boise for my scheduled dance lessons without feeling rushed. I said goodbye to the mountain range which is called the Crazy Mountains, one of its peaks reaching into the sky over 11,000 feet in elevation. The mountain range surrounded the town and felt like they were giving the town a little hug.

Continuing to Idaho my next stop was Bozeman, Montana, which was certainly not as quaint but had more activity. I treated myself to a luxury hotel in Bozeman. The hotel had it all. There were two restaurants, a nightclub with live music, a rooftop pool, and it was in the center of the main strip through town. I sure needed the break from moving each day to a new spot. I needed rest from the uncertainty of where I would stay the next night. I did love the spontaneity and the adventure, but I also needed a moment of security and this was a great place for that. I found some dancing in town and made a few friends.

With the help of some local folks that I struck up random conversation with at the nightclub, I found my way to a small watering hole where the local people were more than willing to welcome me into their crowd. I found a few dance partners and experienced the local life. An adorable elderly couple were swing-dancing their hearts out. They were entirely in sync, step per step and clearly in love. I took a video on my phone. When their dances were done I showed them the video in which I also caught the most sincere kiss between these life-long lovers. This interaction wound up landing me a dance with the older man. I thanked his wife for allowing me the dance and off we went. Her mister was a solid lead, nothing fancy, no tricks or dips, he led with well educated footwork and clear signals which made me feel like Cinderella on the floor. During the dance he told me that he and his wife learned to swing dance when they were just young things in high school. Apparently country swing dance was part of their phys-ed program back in another time.

At that moment I wished I had grown up in rural Montana. I started thinking about my own days in school. No one in my life today would believe I was the shy girl in school. In elementary school I was always getting in trouble for the enormity of my shyness. I was the girl who would barely speak in class and always tried to hide from getting called on. I don't know exactly when or how the shift happened, but I went from this quiet and shy child to being the one who loved to lead discussions and entice debates in college. I then became someone who could go alone into a random place in a state I've never been in before and make friends every time. I am grateful for this growth. I have learned that the statement, "This is just how I am," is a lazy excuse. The work is sometimes hard but how we move forward is altogether in our control. This goes for all of the things that would otherwise hold one back from being one's best self. It applies to taking steps to overcome fears, it applies to picking out people or situations that are not good for us and letting them go. It applies to seeing behaviors, anxieties and excuses in ourselves that are not in our best interest and finding the strength and courage to change them.

After two days of balancing dancing, resting from the road, and soaking in the rooftop pool overlooking the Rocky Mountains, I decided it was time to head for Yellowstone. It was a short two hour drive from Bozeman before I started seeing the signs that said "Stay alert for bison crossing."

I followed the advice of the woman in Casper, Wyoming, deciding on the route to Yellowstone that avoided the mountain passes. Although working on my fear of heights, I needed a break. I forgave myself for this and thought, "Clearly it is a process of peaks and valleys," giggling out loud thinking, "Pun intended." I could press through if I had to but the outcome did not meet the risk for me in this particular situation as it had when I went to see Christine.

I realized this was a fantastic decision and the perfect route to get there. It was easy and relaxing. I danced in the driver seat to country music and admired nature through the windows. I felt excitement grow as I pulled up to the towering row of tolls at the entrance to Yellowstone National Park. I rolled up to the toll booth window and the park ranger took my payment then handed me a map with warnings about wild animals and thermal pools.

Proceeding into the park it hit me. I'm in Yellowstone National Park! It was amazing! Now if only I can find a bison. I so wanted a bison sighting. I had no idea the abundance of these majestic creatures in this remarkable, mystical place. Soon I would understand why so many people said to me, "There's no way you won't see bison." The excitement that flowed through my blood when I saw my first one is indescribable. This enormous, imperial animal climbed out of the awe-inspiring Yellowstone River and walked alongside the Chevy. The wild beast glanced at me with his deeply soulful, glistening brown eyes, holding the eye contact just long enough to forge a connection between us that, to me, was palpable. I will never forget that feeling.

I continued my drive through the park for approximately thirty minutes before I reached Old Faithful. Along my drive I was at a loss for words, enamored by the enchantment of the steel-colored, snow-capped Rocky Mountains in the background. The mountains overlook the winding and flowing Yellowstone River, mesmerizing through the lush green fields. Words can't describe this and pictures can't capture the formidable magnificence. There's no way to communicate the feeling of merely existing under the big Montana sky and time frozen in only that moment. The rest of life just falls away and there is a deeply spiritual connection between a soul and the spectacular marvel of the earth.

Old Faithful lived up to its name. I got there long before the predicted eruption so I had time to walk the curving walkways and boardwalks around the thermal pools, seeing the natural beauty while getting some exercise. The geyser was right on time. When the post eruption applause ended I sauntered back to my truck and after crossing from Wyoming where Old Faithful was back into the Montana section of the park, I exited the way I entered, through West Yellowstone. Within minutes I crossed the Idaho State line. I had no idea what was next so I called Elise for her help on the matter. I was due in Boise for dance lessons in two days so I had time to see more before I had to be there.

Chapter 11

What Next?

My adventurous side was yearning for more. There were several towns to stop in before I reached Boise and after talking to Elise I knew they were safe places to visit. The first town she recommended was Idaho Falls. This is a super cute little town and by the time I got there I was a little bit tired and definitely hungry, so I looked for some nearby restaurants online and made a decision. I figured I would sit at the bar and talk to some locals and see what was going on, which has worked for me most every time I've dropped in on an unfamiliar place. It was a Friday so there had to be something happening. My last text message to Elise was this: "I just looked, it's a four-hour drive to Boise and I've already driven like eight hours today so I think I'm gonna just sleep here in Idaho Falls and I'll get there by noon or one tomorrow."

Although I had high hopes when I walked into the restaurant, the conversations didn't turn up much. It didn't seem that there was a lot going on in this town and the things that were going on didn't really interest me. After a meal and a rest at the bar I decided to move on and get closer to Boise. On the way, I wanted to go to a compelling tourist attraction called Craters of the Moon, which sounded fascinating. To get there I would have to travel west on Route 26, and to continue from Craters to Boise I would take Route 20 West until reaching Interstate 84.

Some research on the topography map revealed that there might be a scary stretch of road and after all the driving I'd done today, I was too tired and I really wasn't in the mood to challenge myself to that extent. I made the difficult decision to skip making that stop and head south to get to Boise via another small town Elise and I had discussed. I decided it was best to avoid the mountainous regions for this day and pick up stretching out of my comfort zone again after Boise. I arrived in Pocatello and was instantly disappointed.

Pocatello is even smaller than Idaho Falls and there was absolutely nothing of interest to me there. I found no historical sites, no museums, no visitor center, not even a quaint small downtown atmosphere. After a few minutes of driving around I didn't see any friendly or welcoming people to strike up a conversation with. At this point I was only a couple of hours from Boise. If I continued and arrived tonight I could dance since it was Friday and also get an additional bonus dance night tomorrow. Wednesdays and weekends are the best nights at the club where Elise and Troy teach dance lessons.

The prospect of seeing my friends for an extra couple of days and dancing all weekend made the additional hours of driving more appealing. That seemed like the best answer for me as now the failed attempt of my last two stops had me all adventured-out for the day. My new plan was to try to get there and if I got too tired I could always try to find a hotel to stop at. I knew I was risking another uncomfortable night of sleeping in the truck. What I have learned about the Midwest is that there is a lot of space and it's possible I would not find a hotel between Pocatello and Boise.

I didn't tell Elise and Troy about my decision to arrive tonight. My next text to Elise was this, "I just parked outside the club!"

Chapter 12

After Idaho

My friend Shelly, who with her military husband has lived all over the world, recently settled in Mississippi. She would fly in and meet me in Idaho and experience some of the West with me. Elise also decided she would love to join us for a few days. So, it was decided.

I just had the most amazing week of social dancing and lessons at Dirt Road Dancing. Elise and Troy are the most talented and patient instructors who always have the goal of making their students feel successful while creating the most fun and effective environment to learn in. I love their lessons and even more importantly, their friendship. I so enjoy visiting with all of my Idaho friends. Elise joining this quest for a few days made leaving my beloved Boise a little bit less somber. I was happy that I didn't have to say goodbye to her just yet.

The three of us girls, Elise, Shelly and I, took off on our way south, deciding on the quicker and flatter Nevada route in lieu of the much more scenic but yet slower and scarier Utah mountain passes. It was a fine choice.

We took Interstate 84 leaving Boise and followed it all the way to Twin Falls, Idaho. In Twin Falls we picked up 93 southbound. We crossed the Perrine Bridge over Snake River Canyon. I was very proud of myself for driving over the bridge of 486 feet in height with no reaction at all.

Directly on the other side of the bridge was the visitor center. After two hours of road time, all three of us needed the ladies room, so we made a stop.

Upon exiting the visitor center building and heading back to my truck, we noticed something strange. A group of people were putting on harnesses and helmets next to the parking lot. We speculated as to what they were doing and we figured it out as the group started walking out onto the bridge wearing backpacks. Of course we had to stay for the excitement! We didn't know before now that this was a popular base jumping site and we felt very lucky to happen upon the action.

We had our fill of watching the thrill seekers climb one at a time over the rails, take their leap of faith and smoothly sail downward to the riverbank one by one.

We watched about five or six jumps and then resolved to carry on our way. Approaching the truck we noticed a carved stone monument sign. Here we learned another interesting fact about Snake River Canyon that day. Evel Knievel had once attempted a famous jump at this location. The jump failed due to a faulty parachute that deployed too early; thankfully Evel walked away unscathed. The stone monument reads as such: "Robert Evel Knievel Explorer Motorcyclist and Daredevil attempted a mile long leap of the Snake River Canyon on Sept. 8, 1974 Employing a unique skycycle. The large dirt ramp is visible approx. 2 Miles east of this point on the south ridge of the canyon."

The drive through Nevada provided vast stretches of absolutely nothing peppered with the occasional Alien-themed tourist trap. We passed the time joking, laughing and also sharing stories of ourselves, our pasts and our present situations. Total girl-bonding time, there is nothing else like it.

After nine fun yet tiring hours on the road, we decided to do an overnight rest in Las Vegas. While Shelly recharged in the room, Elise and I found some boot-stomping fun at the famous Stoney's Las Vegas Country and Western nightclub. We spun, we stomped, we two-stepped until our dance bug was satisfied, we then retreated to the hotel to sleep for a few hours before our drive to

Phoenix. Shelly and I managed to squeeze in a morning hike before leaving Las Vegas.

Chapter 13

The Jail Tree

We were cruising along Route 93 to Phoenix to dance at the popular country music club Denim and Diamonds. Elise and I were excited to dance with some people that we knew through the dance community online. I was most excited that I would finally meet and dance with the famous YouTube dancer who I had reached out to ahead of time. Shelly was most excited to have the hotel room to herself while Elise and I kicked our heels up. Shelly loves reading. The solitude of the quiet hotel room and a good book will recharge her soul the way country tunes, spins and dips do for Elise and me.

Still about an hour outside of Phoenix, we saw a sign that said Wickenburg, Arizona. Elise suddenly got excited. "Look! Wickenburg! I've always wanted to stop in Wickenburg. It's an old cowboy town and it has a lot to offer! We should definitely stop there and check it out!," she exclaimed.

Wickenburg is a fascinating Arizona town established in 1863. It definitely caught my attention as there are several signs and many statues commemorating renowned cowgirls and other Western philanthropists, entrepreneurs, and heroes. Strategically placed and colorfully painted, the statues tell the tale of a wilder West and the impact that each individual had on history. Some of the statues talked to you. The technology is simple: push a button to hear the recorded eye-opening account of the individual's life and experiences.

As you wander around the town between cactuses of all shapes and sizes, you will see an old train and several small-town shops that take you back through time. Overhead banners promote an event celebrating cowgirls outside of Desert Caballeros Western Museum.

Learning about Barrel cacti, Saguaro (the big tree-like cacti that you often see in cartoons), and prickly pear cacti was cool. I enjoyed reading the informative signs about the history of Locomotive 761. The 1890's classic train engine car sat proudly outside the station house which had been cleverly transformed into the visitor center. I could imagine myself on the platform around the late 1890's through the mid 1900's. The conductor, proudly clad in his freshly pressed jacket adorned with shining, well-polished buttons, and on his head his distinctive railroad hat, would call, "All aboard," in a deep authoritative voice. The train would hiss as the engineer relaxed an arm on the ledge of the window while the huge black steel engine, equipped with bell and cowcatcher, chugged forward with steam billowing from the towering stack.

I think the most interesting historical site in Wickenburg is an old mesquite tree, still standing strong and proud. This tree served as the jail. A statue of an inmate chained to the tree takes the viewer back to a time that would leave modern social activists horrified. A journey into the criminal-justice history of

Wickenburg from 1863 to 1890 reveals that in this time there was no proper facility in which to house those accused of criminal activity and awaiting trial. Instead, the accused were chained to what is famously known as the Jail Tree. While awaiting a proper lawman to collect them and take them to a proper jail in the larger city of Phoenix, an inmate was at the mercy of the elements. As the history goes, no inmate ever escaped the Jail Tree.

Thinking about the poor troubled souls that sat chained to the Jail Tree, I imagined their regret. This made me examine my own life and sorrowful moments that I could choose to look at as regrets. I realize that regret is a useless emotion. It doesn't necessarily result in growth and it doesn't promote change. Change and growth occur when one takes what could be just a mistake and instead of regret, chooses to see the lesson. I've had many such lessons. I do however have one regret. Many years before I sold my home, my then-teenage son had moved into the basement of my house. At this time my father, the architect, offered to install a bathroom for my son in the basement. He asked me if I would like it to be a half bath or a full bath. I thought about it and told him I didn't want to take advantage of his generosity, so let's just do a half bath. My son was perfectly capable of walking up the stairs to get a shower and the half bath would prevent his friends from coming up into the main part of the house to use the restroom when they were visiting him, affording me my precious privacy. He would also be able to use the restroom in the middle of the night without having to walk up two flights of stairs.

My father encouraged me to take the full bath but I was unwilling to have him put in what I thought was more effort. I thanked him and said I'll take the half bath. I regret that. That is my one regret. I should've taken the full bath. When I went to sell the house it would've definitely been worth more with what would've been an in-law suite if I had the full bathroom. Everything else is a lesson. Everything else I have an opportunity to improve on and change moving forward, however this was the only house that I would ever be selling and I have no opportunity or room for improvement in this situation. This is a regret. I can live with it.

Our time in Phoenix was fun. The days were spent hiking with Shelly in the San Tan Mountain Regional Park in Queen Creek, Arizona. This was my first true desert hike. The cacti were spectacular and the animals were so much fun. We saw Arizona Striped Whiptail lizards in abundance, they were hard to see at first because they are fast, tiny and blend well with their surroundings. Once you see the speedy little buggers the first time you will then notice them everywhere. We saw several species of birds feeding happily on prickly pear fruit. A not-so-adorable lizard also lives in these parts, the Gila monster! These creatures are very scary, appropriately cloaked in Halloween colors of black and orange. They are the only venomous lizard native to the United States and will open their mouths exposing up to 45 very sharp teeth and then hiss at you in warning of the bite that you will want to avoid. The Gila monster does not inject their poison like a snake would, instead they latch onto their victim and chew the flesh to infuse their poisonous neurotoxin into the capillary system. Shelly thought it was cute to find the most terrifying picture of this reptile to show me just before we entered the trail. "That's what friends are for," she informed me, amused by my horror. We enjoyed several trails including one called the Stargazer Trail and thankfully no Gila monster encounters. After the hike, a shower and a rest before the night was danced away with Elise at the honky-tonk.

Chapter 14

Sedona 89 to Flagstaff 66

Next up was Sedona. The three of us decided this was a great little side trip and it was also convenient to get to Route 66 from there, which was something I really wanted to experience. We decided on spending a day in Sedona and I knew the roads were going to be challenging. I was rested and recovered from the earlier parts of the trip and decided I was fine to drive. I'm so glad that I had the support of these two girls. Whenever the road would get hairy, they would just start talking to me about just about anything, distracting me and I could breathe through it. And I was able to continue to pilot the Chevy over some sizable mountain passes. I was even able to look at the scenery from time to time and could admire the beauty, though it would be a stretch to say I was enjoying it. All of the clichés applied: baby steps, slow and steady wins the race, keep on truckin'. I was making strides. It helped that the girls were not concerned. They had faith in me to keep all of us safe and so therefore I felt confident.

The two-hour drive was mostly a straight shot up Interstate 17, a short stint on scenic Route 179. We knew we were almost to Sedona when we saw the sign for Arizona Route 89.

Another friend of Elise's from Boise was in the area and met us in Sedona to spend the day with us. The two of them would drive back to Idaho together. At the end of the day,

Shelly and I wished the two of them safe travels and I had a tearful "See you later" with Elise.

Once Shelly and I were back on the road, I thought, "Wow, God was really watching out for me again." Even with all of the advances I had been making with heights, I absolutely would never have been able to drive Route 89A North from Sedona to Flagstaff. I have been working hard on overcoming my fear, yet my acrophobia won this round. On this narrow stretch of road on the edge of a canyon is the most amazing and beautiful scenery (so I have been told). I don't really know because I can't even look. I had to keep my eyes closed and distract myself by talking to my son on the phone while Shelly navigated this dangerous section of roadway. I am so grateful for the fact that she decided that this was the part of my trip she wanted to join me for. I never realized how much I would need her help when my friend reached out to me and expressed how she understood that I really wanted to do this trip on my own but would it be okay for her to accompany me for a few days to see some of the West and to hike. If I were on my own for this challenging section of road, I have no idea how I would have handled it. I have come a long way in the past weeks, but still far from considering myself cured. I started out behind the wheel, we didn't know until we got moving what this highway was like. In the first few minutes after leaving Sedona I was feeling only excitement, I couldn't wait to explore Historic Route 66. Shortly into the trek I became lightheaded. No shoulder, no guardrail, and hundreds, maybe a thousand feet, down into the canyon on my right. One narrow lane each direction and plenty of curves had my hands sweating, my head spinning and my stomach turning. I pulled into a small parking lot belonging to a trailhead to my left and that's when my good friend stepped in to help me through it. I jumped out of the truck, caught my breath and Shelly got behind the wheel for the next twenty-eight miles until we reached the Flagstaff Visitor's Center.

We spotted a couple of javelinas poking their noses out of the brush and then emerging by the trailhead. These aggressive wild hogs were on our list of hoped-for animal sightings but preferably from afar.

Javelinas were another animal which Shelly had fun torturing me with over pictures of angry-face peccaries and the severe wounds they caused. Shelly enlightened me with stories of these wild pigs brutalizing hikers with their razor-sharp tusks and attacking in large squadrons. As it turns out this is a very rare occurrence and usually associated with people trying to feed them or otherwise approach them not understanding the importance of distance when they encounter wild animals. One distinctive warning that javelinas are nearby is their putrid odor. One might think they are about to happen upon a surfeit of skunks.

Even though she liked ribbing me about the dangers of the desert animals, I enjoyed Shelly's company tremendously. She is an incredibly independent woman, and I knew she would be a fantastic complement to what

I was doing out here. The fact that she respected my need for independence made her the perfect companion for a few days of hiking and exploring. Her ability to navigate these dangerous roads was no more than a bonus.

Although my cross-country experience was quite different, I think I get my sense of adventure from my father. He was a young man when he left for California on a whim. He tried for several years to make a life there.

Like so many others, my father was drafted into the army during the Vietnam War. He was one of the lucky ones, he got to stay stateside. He spent the wartime working as an aircraft mechanic, stationed at Fort Benning in Georgia. After his time in the army was done, my dad packed up his few belongings and took leave from Pennsylvania for California. He secured a job as a garbage-truck salesman and had high aspirations for a western lifestyle.

Not only is my father adventurous, he is also resourceful, with an unusual sense of humor. After several years, life in California did not work out as he had hoped. He decided to come back to the East Coast where he was more familiar and had more opportunities. Fueled by several disappointments in California including the closure of the garbage-truck company, my father developed his insatiable work ethic. I would fortunately, and also unfortunately, inherit this trait as well.

At this time he still didn't have much money and he was quite aware that his current

only option he could find. It was a different world in 1968; first, no security cameras. Believe it or not my dad is one of the most honest and respectful people that I know. My father always does right by people and has a fantastic sense of what is fair. He went on to be a successful man, helping many others along the way. He long made up for this one unavoidable indiscretion with a lifetime of good deeds and compassionate acts.

There it was sitting at over 6900 feet in elevation! I took a picture of the first evidence that we were on Route 66–a huge white and blue depiction of the shield-shaped route sign painted on the road outside the Tudor-style visitors' center. I was distracted for a moment by a guy with headphones dancing in the parking lot by himself. He was clearly enjoying the music and his life, perhaps not in that order. I admired him.

"Are we going or are we just going to stay here tonight?" Shelly's jesting sarcasm prompted me to stop videoing the dancing man and put my attention back on the task of conquering the Mother Road.

The first true Route 66 landmark that we came across was the ruins of Twin Arrows Gas Station and Trading Post. The once bold red and bright gold arrows now stood in disrepair with faded paint, splintered wood and a missing arrowhead. The fuel pumps still stood in front of the graffiti-covered building, barely visible in the tangles of weeds growing unrestrainedly. What was once a busy trading post visited daily by so many transcontinental travelers looking to fuel up and find a cool drink and a souvenir, was now an echo from the past.

When traveling the Main Street of America, jumping on and off of Route 40 is necessary because only about 85 percent of 66 is still drivable. In its glory days, 66 carried hundreds of thousands of motorists and depression-era migrants and so many others over the decades from the Midwest to California. Reducing travelers' trips by over 200 miles for fifty-nine years, Route 66 entered the realm of history. On June 27, 1985, the iconic road succumbed to the more modern, wider and faster interstate system when the American Association of State Highway and Transportation officials decertified the road and voted to remove all its highway signs.

Keeping an eye out for the small brown historic Route 66 signs that replaced the original, much larger, highway signs can be tricky. They are easy to miss. We got pretty good at spotting them as the days went on.

Our next find was in the ghost town of Coconino County, Arizona. Meteor City Trading Post sat deserted and lonely. This legendary Route 66 landmark is known for its giant roadside dreamcatcher and its geodesic dome sporting a giant yellow mohawk. At one time tourists visited it in droves. They would explore the concrete teepees and purchase keepsakes such as petrified rocks and Native American goods. Now it sits dilapidated, just a ghost of its former alluring brilliance.

Next stop: Winslow, Arizona, where I took a picture next to a flatbed Ford and then a quick jaunt around the Take it Easy Corner where if you look closely you may see some scandalous activity painted into a second-story window.

Moving on, we found ourselves in Joseph City. Not sure if this is a famous stop but it was certainly interesting to see the pioneer museum, though it was closed. "It seems my travels are beset by closed museums," I giggled to myself at this thought. Peering through the locked wrought-iron gates, we saw many fun and interesting pieces of farming history.

We kept on going. We saw the famous Wigwam Motel in Holbrook. The most impressive antique cars were parked outside of the individual teepee motel rooms as though the road-weary drivers were still resting inside.

The petrified forest was anticlimactic, however continuing through to the painted desert left me speechless. One thing that happens when you go into an area of the country that is uninhabited by people: You are surrounded by pure and utter silence. I can only describe this silence with the word deafening. A silence so bold and so loud is the only way I know how to describe it. You hear absolutely nothing, everything is still, no radiant sound. I never knew what that sounded like before. I thought I knew what quiet was until this day.

I looked over the unique landscape and all of the colors in the sediment and imagined Native Americans on their horses navigating their way through the unceasing, disorienting and unforgiving desert terrain. A settler crossing toward the West Coast might think they had accidentally wandered off of Earth and onto another planet. It was definitely unearthly. It's difficult to imagine what it was like to be here in the time before the road was carved out for modern tourists, although this place is mostly as it was, natural and raw except for the one road. The low croak of a gigantic raven brought my imagination back to our planet.

Shelly stayed with me through Amarillo, Texas. The slow progression from Arizona through New Mexico made it possible to see so many pieces of American history, including wild horses in the forgotten town of Gallup. Here we saw the most incredible sunset during a scary moment of getting lost on a deserted desert road. We had no cell or GPS signal, we were low on fuel and losing light quickly. The sun sets much faster in the west than in the east. Shelly had a moment of extreme discomfort bordering on panic. I wasn't worried. I had planned for such a disadvantageous event. I told her that if it turned out that we had to sleep in the truck, I had everything we needed. I had blankets, pillows, water, toilet paper, camping meals, a camping stove and lighters. I had batteries, flashlights, and bear spray in case we needed to deal with any animals (bear spray works on more than bears). I was prepared, Shelly was not impressed. We did finally find our way back to 40 and a modern hotel before the fuel ran out.

The day after Gallup, we took a more mainstream detour to the beautiful old city of Albuquerque and spent a day visiting wineries and adorable little shops.

After seven days together our last stop was the famous Route 66 Cadillac Ranch. The ranch is nothing more than a westward line of cars partially buried nose down in an endless empty field beside old 66. The simple expression of Americana brings a creative enchantment to this stretch of road. I climbed up onto one of the old graffiti-covered Cadillacs and stood there just staring out over the Texas prairieland.

I felt so free.

Chapter 15

Don't Mess with Texas

Outside the Amarillo airport, my parting with Shelly was not as dispiriting as it could have been because I knew I was going to see her again a week from now in Mississippi. We had a cleverly devised plan to soak up as much distal adventure as possible, albeit this short separation. I was looking forward to seeing her again after Texas.

With no exact plan now that I was once again on my own, campaigning for adventure and experience, I had only the idea that I wanted to dance in Houston after talking to Alex. I have been keeping in touch with Alex, that young hottie from Roanoke Virginia. We have been staying connected since that first night of my trip with text messages from time to time. He encouraged me to try the dancing scene in Houston. I figured that I would go check out Houston via Lubbock, Texas, because there was someone there that I needed to stop and see.

I loosely planned that my route after Texas would be to travel east along the gulf coast through Louisiana, Ocean Springs, Mississippi, for Shelly and then into Pensacola, Florida. I had heard about the famous beach bar called Flora-Bama and I hoped I would find some dancing there. Houston was on my radar but before that could happen I was so close to Dallas that there was no way I wouldn't try to see my friend Tess.

One thing my deeply observant friends have pointed out to me over the years is that networking is my superpower. I instinctively collect connections, acquaintanceships and friendships with individuals who have unique skills and gifts. Whenever somebody is discussing something, looking for help with something or could benefit from a connection with someone, I can always say I have a person for that. It's always someone I trust with whom I've established a mutual admiration. I may not know all of them well, but early on I detect genuine talent. I have a knack for picking up unquestionably well on who is good at what they do.

This skill is what made me a great horse-farm manager for the ten years I did that. So many people who manage horse farms think they need to know how to do everything. They think they need to be a Jack-of-all-trades related to horses. This just isn't possible. My feeling is, as a manager my job is to be the very best manager. What makes me the best at that is *not* knowing how to do everything, it's knowing who is precisely the best person to call. Who are the best professional nutritionists and the best farriers and the best vets and the best saddle fitters and so on. I'm blessed to have this talent and I tend to know someone for everything. I collect the most wonderful people.

In Lubbock, Texas, there was Travis. I don't know why or how but I just knew I could trust him. Travis Salsman is a career truck driver from Texas who I'd never met in person. I became friends with Travis on

Facebook. I don't know how it happened or how he wound up in my newsfeed but I'm so glad that he did. He's a distinctly interesting person. First, all of his coast-to-coast trucking adventures that he would share on social media were intriguing to me. I enjoyed reading them on the regular. The other thing he does which is important and interesting is that he has an organization called Make Peace With Police. The mission of this organization is to bridge the gap between police and the community by promoting education, understanding and compassion. Travis helps to forge relationships which otherwise wouldn't have been developed. Such a great cause!

When I was planning this trip I got valuable advice from Travis and anytime I ran into trouble I was able to give him a call to help me figure out whatever I need to know about the road. When Shelly and I were leaving New Mexico and heading for Texas I was concerned about mountain passes again. I reached out to him to find out what to expect or prepare for. Travis informed me I had nothing to be worried about, I would discover only tame roads in that region. Knowing what was ahead made the drive so much more relaxing.

It became particularly important to me to meet Travis. I knew that he would be a friend for a long, long time. I organized with Travis to meet him for lunch in Lubbock on my way from Amarillo to Dallas to see Tess.

Tess is a good friend of mine from a small quaint Texas town outside of Dallas called Burleson. I met her by chance, or perhaps divine intervention, one random day in line at a convenience store near my home. While waiting to pay for my coffee I heard someone behind me make a comment in a warm and gentle voice with the most beautiful of southern accents. I turned around and saw a lovely, cheerful young woman and I said, "I bet you're not from around here."

"How did you know?" she playfully responded with a shy smile that brightened the room. I can't remember what her exact comment was that caused me to turn around in the first place, but I'm so glad that she said it. We have been friends ever since.

It was a man that originally brought Tess to Pennsylvania. Unfortunately, it was a tumultuous relationship and my beautiful friend gave it more time than it deserved. It was a scary day when she left the clearly unstable man, but she managed to get out unscathed.

Tess made her plans to move back to Texas after a short stretch of staying in my guestroom. I'd only gotten to see her one time since her move several years ago. Now, here I was in Texas, I had the time, so I called her.

"Tess, I can't be here in Texas and not see you!" I announced as she answered the phone. Her reply was quick. "My guest room that you stayed in last time isn't available, I'm using it for storage but come here and stay with me tonight, we will find a way to make it work out." So I did.

We had the most magnificent reunion. We hugged like we hadn't seen each other in decades and we talked like we hadn't missed a day.

Tess convinced me to stay a second night. Night number two was quite the riot! Tess invited me to join her for some fun at one of her girlfriends' homes. It was an interesting gathering, exercising the new millennium's answer to the antiquated era of Tupperware parties–high-end sex toy parties.

Instead of a modestly dressed homemaker explaining the perfect airtight seal on the latest piece of plasticware that promises to keep your leftover meatloaf fresh for a week, we are now being lectured by a red-lipstick wearing, curvy woman in strappy high heels, about ten speeds, multiple-vibration patterns and clitoral stimulation. All sizes, shapes and colors, some of them even light up and most of them are waterproof for fun in the bath or shower.

It was about two hours of perfectly inappropriate jokes, authentic laughter, and questions from the peanut gallery such as, "Will this one be guaranteed to make my vagina happy?" The thirty minutes following the hysterical demonstrations were spent placing orders, followed by an evening swim in the hostess's pool.

Funny vibrator party aside, I'm so glad that I stayed and spent that time with Tess. One thing I've been realizing lately is you take the time when you can for the people you love. It's cliché to say it but it's so true that you never know when it will be the last time, so love them today.

I don't know why but my own mortality
had recently become much more of a reality
to me. I think it might be partially because of
the loss of a long-time friend just a few years
earlier. In the moment I learned that Jay had
passed, something changed inside me. He was
the one friend that there was no way anything
could happen to. He not only lived life but the
guy grabbed life by the horns and rode the
hell out of it! He did things people only
dream of. Amongst many other successes, the
man actually moved to Los Angeles and
became a rock star!

Jay's passing was for sure a huge
contributor to my readiness to hear what Jesse
was saying to me that day in the pub. Each
day that goes on I seem to have more
awakenings.

After my time with Tess, I was ready to head for Houston. The drive was fine and sometimes scenic. I went through parts that were east of the beautiful Texas Hill Country but could easily be mistaken for such.

I looked up the best places to stay near Houston and I decided to stay in the Katy area. I had no trouble finding a hotel.

That night with Alex's text-message input, I settled on dancing at a place called Whiskey River West. I showed up early, just when the doors were opening. It can be very difficult to be a stranger in a local dancing scene and getting dances is sometimes next to impossible since these places can be very cliquey. Knowing this, I wanted to get there before it got crowded and before things started going full swing. I went in and made small talk with a couple of the waitresses and jumped in on a couple of mechanical bull ride rounds with them. This encounter turned out to be a fantastic idea. These girls knew most of the dancers and were able to introduce me to a few leads throughout the night. The other strategy I had for landing some dances was from the great advice of my Idaho friend, Elise. Elise taught me that if you're having trouble getting a dance then you should look around the room and find the oldest man in the place. She informed me that it would be very unlikely that the oldest man would ever turn down a dance if you requested it from him. Once everybody else sees you out on the floor then they will start to ask you for dances or say yes when you ask them. Another very important piece of information I learned from Elise was never turn a dance down. As soon as you say no, anyone who notices this will not ask you for a dance. This advice proved to be sound and true. Dancing with the oldest man on the floor worked like a charm. I had a great night in Houston and the next day I was ready for my drive along the southern Gulf Coast.

Chapter 16

Shelly, Carl and Some Tall Bridges

It was about a seven-hour drive from Katy, Texas, to Ocean Springs, Mississippi, where I would get to see Shelly once again. The drive took me through Louisiana. I had been to New Orleans in the past. The experiences there at those times made me realize this was just a drive-through state for me, there was no inspiration there for me to make a stop. I did stop for fuel even though I didn't really need it, just to touch my feet to the ground and add another state to the list of states that I visited on this peregrination. One positive I can surely say about Louisiana is driving the raised highway. Traveling Interstate 10 the whole way along the coast I would cross through the bayou of southern Louisiana. This impressive, elevated roadway is fascinating and the landscape has an eerie uniqueness that is inexplicably beautiful. I thought about the alligator population, two-million strong, residing throughout the state and in the swamps below. So cool! They were great at concealing themselves in the overgrown marsh. I didn't spot any of these magnificent yet dangerous creatures, but I knew they were there.

It must have been my reptilian daydreams that caused me to miss the bypass going through New Orleans. The local route has a series of very high, very narrow bridges that when looking at them from the approach seem incredibly intimidating to even those without my phobia. I was ready for it. I was going over these bridges and I wasn't going to get upset about it. I was happy for the opportunity to test the improvements I've made. I was well rested after my night spent in Shelly's comfortable guest room and prepared to handle it without excess stress. I was proud of myself after I made it through this section of roadway with very little anxiety.

What a cute little town, I thought as I crossed over into Ocean Springs, Mississippi. The line of shrimping boats in the small inlet reminded me of a very popular 90's movie. Such an interesting place. Very much small-town America, but with a beach and a massive amount of humidity to boot. Ocean Springs has a quaint downtown with small boutique stores, adorable bakeries and all of the southern charm you could hope for. One of my favorite things about Ocean Springs is that the town has affectionately adopted several stray chickens and roosters. The most popular rooster was fondly named Carl, he was known throughout the town and beyond. Shelly and I were lucky enough to be joined by Carl for breakfast while we sat outside a tiny bakery café and shared our bagels with him. Carl seemed to be quite grateful until we ran out of food and then he abandoned us, moving on to other cafés down the road. That's okay, we didn't take it personally. Well, maybe just a little.

Shelly and I spent some time exploring downtown and later took a walk in a park where we were lucky enough to see a small alligator sunning itself on the cool damp stones above the murky waters and tall reeds of the vast swampland. We enjoyed him from a safe distance.

The best part of seeing Shelly again was relaxing with her at her beautiful modern condo home amongst the company of her three pet birds, all of which are full of comic personality.

Spending time, walking with her talking, and just being in her company is cathartic. Conversations between true-blue female friends who honestly care about one another always contain good nutrient-rich verbiage that feeds and provides nourishment to the soul.

Chapter 17

Beach Bars, Banjos and New Friends

I was not exactly sure how the next few days would go, what I did know was that leaving Shelly's I was bound for Pensacola and Flora-Bama Beach Bar. This legendary establishment sits right on the stateline separating Orange Beach, Alabama, and Perdido Key, Florida, hence the catchy Flora-Bama name. Of course, at Flora-Bama one will find beach concerts, oceanside triathlons, the annual Chili Cook-off, and even a January Polar Bear Dip, however this venue is more infamously known for its quirky idiosyncratic events. Sadly, I was not there at the right time to catch the Boozy Adult Spelling Bee, the Bulls on the Beach Rodeo, or what could possibly be their most anticipated annual event, the Interstate Mullet Toss & Beach Party.

It was a rainy day and not much was happening. I would have stayed another day to experience this place in the sun, but I ran into a problem with that. I was surprised to discover that June was an indubitably popular time in the Florida panhandle. I always assumed Florida vacation time was the winter and quickly learned that this was not true of the panhandle. It was slightly reminiscent of the southern Jersey shore in summertime. Apparently, this far north in Florida, summer is the time to be here and because I had no reservation, I was unable to find a hotel room anywhere within twenty miles. Every single room was sold out.

When I got to Flora-Bama and learned this dilemma, my thought was that if I was having fun there I would stay until 10 or 11 PM and then drive an hour or two east to find a hotel room outside of the vacation area. That would have been my choice, but because of the rain I made the decision to move on sooner. I learned that my plan would not have worked very well anyway. There was literally nothing an hour or two east of Perdido key.

The Florida panhandle is very rural. It was not uninhabited like Oklahoma—I felt much safer in Oklahoma. The panhandle was just rural enough to have a good amount of poverty and the sinister dueling banjos ambiance of the movie Deliverance.

I think I pinpointed one of the most profound changes that happened inside of myself in recent years but only realized it during the last five weeks on the road, especially in the weeks which were spent on my own. Some new type of tranquility has become the prevalent reaction when I encounter things that may make other people, including my former self, anxious or even panicked. Things that would've made me upset now seem to cause me to think in a more focused way. Calm and slow. I've always seen myself as a problem solver with more of a fight than flight instinct, however this focused calm in moments of concern is new. This drive through the Florida panhandle proved it. I knew I was not safe here alone. I knew it would be unsafe to sleep in my truck. It was getting dark, I was getting very tired and I hadn't eaten since I left Mississippi this morning. I needed to find food and a place to lay my head down and there was nothing except for Florida brush and swamp in every direction. The exits only came about every thirty to forty miles.

I was traveling toward Ocala to visit my friend Brittany Yard. Brittany is a long-time friend from the horse world. She is as talented a rider, competitor, horse trainer and coach as she is a spectacular friend. Brittany had recently moved her business, Square One Equestrian, from Frenchtown, New Jersey, to Ocala, Florida, where she was able to submerge herself in year-round equine activity without the interruption of harsh northern New Jersey winters. The Ocala equine community was large, active and competitive.

It was a wonderful place for her to advance her business and showcase her talent.

I had spoken with Brittany just as I was leaving the Pensacola area and I told her I was en route. She was excited to see me and wanted me to visit for a few days. I was equally excited to see her and spend those days with her. I knew I could only stay a few days because as strange as it felt to consider this, it was time to start thinking about going home. I committed to a work schedule starting July fifth and it was now the last week of June. I didn't want this time in the great wide open to end, I shook away the thought and became present again. I had gotten pretty good at staying in the moment on this venture. I am not sure when that exceptionally notable shift took place or what solidified it inside me, perhaps the experience in Memphis, maybe the magic of the Rockies. Conceivably, it was just being away and slowing down. Whatever the reason, I'm glad for it. I will commit to continue to practice living in the moment. It creates a much happier and fulfilling existence.

I called Brittany once more while I was driving through the panhandle and let her know my situation. I'm still four to five hours from Ocala and at least two hours from Tallahassee where I know there will be a hotel. I don't think I have another two hours in me right now.

I'm seeing occasional exits for small towns but I don't know what they're like or how safe they are, so I put Brittany on the task of doing the research for me. I was driving and did not feel good about pulling over to do the research myself for several reasons. I didn't feel safe stopping there but more importantly, I wanted to keep moving because of how tired I was getting and wanted the best chance to get as close as possible to whatever Brittany would find for me.

As I was waiting for her call back my mind went internal again, just as it had in Oklahoma. In my thoughts I reviewed the changes that had happened inside of myself in just five short weeks.

I contemplated how maybe it's okay to let go of parts of myself and my past that I had once believed defined me as a person, just as I would let go of items that are no longer useful. The concept of letting go of pieces of me is essentially the same as what Lenore had taught me about letting go of my house. Maybe holding on to those parts of me only matters if I'm going to live forever. When their time and their usefulness is done, perhaps it's okay to leave them behind. I've learned to leave people who don't bring joy into my life behind. Maybe I need to leave behind elements of my former self that no longer bring me joy. It's a scary concept, but I think it might be okay. Who will I be? Especially when it comes to riding horses. I find myself conflicted because riding horses has always been me, my entire life. I'm no longer enjoying it, yet I continue to force myself to do it. Combine that with who will I be now that I no longer have the piece of me that needs to raise a child? Leaving the equestrian behind would be a choice, unlike leaving the child-raising part of me behind. I don't get a choice in that, after all my son is grown and out on his own and doing his own life now.

I drove around this country east to west now west to east, still wondering where I will find me.

My thoughts were interrupted by the lively music of my cellular ringtone, indicating that Brittany had some information for me. Hitting the answer button on my dashboard computer screen, "Hey there! Do you have a solution for me?"

"Not a great one." Brittany's voice on the other end comforted me slightly but I knew there would still be some issues. "Your best bet is either Chipley or Marianna exits. There are hotels at both of those and each of them has one or two restaurants but unfortunately both are rated extremely high on the danger scale according to the internet."

I took a deep breath, thanked Brittany for her help, and decided I would go to the closer one, Chipley. After Memphis I was much more cognizant of my surroundings and my decision-making process laser focused on safety. I took Exit 120 off of Interstate 10 and instantly felt my heart pounding. I quickly made a U-turn when I saw an angry looking man walking down the middle of the road, his face covered in tattoos. My internal alarm system is on high alert in this unfamiliar, high crime area.

Back on Interstate 10, continuing to Exit 136, I conceded to take my chance in Marianna, Florida. I knew I would have to be careful and I would only get out of the truck once able to park in close proximity to the door of wherever I was going. There were two restaurants sitting side-by-side in a shared parking lot. I chose one and guardedly went inside. The interior of the restaurant was pretty much as expected, modest and marginally clean but it would do. I would grab a quick bite and be on my way. There were several hotels in town. Marianna being one of the only stops for cross-state travelers and truckers explains the exorbitant prices for a room in this tiny, hidden away, precarious little town.

It was busy inside and the only table available was a two-seater high-top table in the back corner of the joint, across from the bar. This was perfect for me because I wanted to be inconspicuous anyway. No such luck–the locals noticed me, clearly not used to passersby stopping in. A few of them looked at me, checking me over but not saying anything. One man sitting at the bar turned around and acknowledged me. I guess I looked out of place and confused or perhaps a little bit out of sorts.

He introduced himself as David and asked me if I was okay. I confided to him that I was concerned about finding a hotel room and that I had been traveling a good part of the day. He told me, here in Marianna it's not the best place for a solo traveler but as long as I choose a hotel that has a lobby and only inside room doors I will be fine. He said avoid the motels with the individual doors on the outside at all costs. He was kind and I knew his advice was of sincere concern for my safety.

I made the calls from the restaurant before venturing to one of the two chain hotels in town that had indoor hallways. I made the calls first because I didn't want to get in and out of my truck too many times. The first one that I called had no rooms available and I began to get nervous. The second one had one last available room and the price was as high as the very fancy Bozeman, Montana, luxury hotel had been. I didn't care. I booked it.

David turned back to me a few minutes later to make sure that I had found something suitable. He seemed genuinely relieved when I told him I found an indoor hotel room. After a meal and securing a room, I was much more relaxed and definitely in a chattier mood. Now I was feeling everything would be fine tonight and I was looking forward to seeing Brittany tomorrow. I stayed another thirty minutes because David and I struck up a conversation. I told him I was on a cross-country journey and I briefly filled him in on many of the adventures behind me over the past weeks. He told me a little bit about himself and shared with me a very personal piece of his health information. I would've never known he was struggling the way that he was by his external demeanor. It just goes to show you never know what somebody is going through. As much as David was dealing with in his own life, his concern that night was for me. The two of us exchanged contact information because he wanted to know when I got out safely the following day and I wanted to know that his health would continue to improve. I wanted to keep in touch, which we would do. We would stay in touch by messages from time to time and an occasional phone call. A year later we would still be friends and probably will be for much longer than that.

The next morning, I checked out of the hotel at the crack of dawn, messaged Brittany that I was only four hours away and steered the Chevy back onto Route 10. About an hour into my drive David called. He wanted to make sure I was safely out of Marianna. He wasn't surprised at all when I told him I left there as soon as the sun came up.

Chapter 18

...and That's a Wrap Folks

It was a joyful reunion with Brittany. We had a wonderful four days together. The time was spent going for walks, going out for the occasional drink, girl talk at Brittany's apartment and lots of time at her farm with her horses. It was so much fun to watch her ride all of them. My favorite thing to watch is the connection between Brittany and her horse Dani, it is sublime poetry. Their ride is a rare dance to music shared only by the two of them. The hot Florida sun does not affect them as they gracefully float around the covered open air arena.

It's now the first week of July and it's time to point the pickup north. It's hard to believe that I am on the last leg of this epic tour. I have gotten used to the road and the nomadic lifestyle. I decided to take my time and make a couple more stops along the way. I settled on Savannah, Georgia, as my next destination.

Savannah was very touristy. Although it wasn't really for me, I can understand the appeal. The brick roads, cute shops, riverfront restaurants and a lovely riverwalk could definitely attract crowds.

I took advantage of the local activities and went on a ghost tour that evening. The next day before checking out I got in a workout. I'd been able to catch a workout at most of the hotels but this one was particularly nice.

I made my best attempt at southern belle attire for this day in southeast Georgia. I chose to wear an adorable yellow eyelet-lace dress that I found in a secondhand shop in Burleson, Texas, while I was visiting Tess. It was perfect for Savannah.

I took a walk on the riverwalk, warm southern summer breeze gently flowing through my hair. I took time out for a drink at one of the riverside bars. Between sips I enjoyed watching the ships sail while casually eavesdropping on the idle conversations of the other travelers around me. I explored interesting hotels along the riverwalk. One of the hotels was exceptionally captivating with an industrial themed interior and some version of a natural-history museum in the lobby and throughout the first floor.

Twenty-four hours was plenty for me in Savannah, so with another day or two left before I had to get back to Pennsylvania I realized I had time to visit some friends who live in Georgia. The two of them are in the animal training business together. They invited me to come and stay when they found out I was in the area. I drove the three and a half hours to see them in Williamson and I spent the next twenty-four hours on their new farm.

They had recently moved from a much more isolated area of Georgia to what was still rural, though more populated and was closer to town. It was beautiful there. I enjoyed catching up with my friends and I loved watching them train their animals. We went out to dinner in the tiny town nearby and in the morning we had big hugs and I departed for the nearly thirteen-hour drive to Pennsylvania.

I drove mostly uninterrupted, except for stopping for an occasional winery or local attraction. Nothing terribly noteworthy, just enough to break up the monotony of the drive and the solemnity of knowing this life-changing chapter is almost over.

Chapter 19

Last Chapter or First Chapter, that is the Question

While driving the faithful pickup that had safely carried me through a lifetime's worth of adventures and lessons compacted into a mere six weeks, I realized I was on Route 95 northbound.

I began to see familiar sites. Looking up I see the welcome sign, Virginia Is For Lovers. It doesn't carry the same euphoric exhilaration as it had in May. Everything in my soul wants to take a hard turn left.

The feeling of melancholy is surrounding me in my truck, I'm swimming in the swampy thickness of it. I can feel the call from the Rockies, their wild spirit beckoning me back. I thought about home. I pondered the question: where is home? I don't really know yet, I only know that my son is in Pennsylvania, my cat misses me, my little apartment comforts me, and my clients rely on me.

Still the Western mountains call to me. My friends, old and new, that are sprinkled out across this great country will be so truly missed. I don't know when I'll see them again. I yearn for them. This trip has answered many questions however opened so many others. Along the journey I realized I still have so much growth to achieve and a lot to learn about who I am and who I can be. It scares me and excites me all at the same time.

This last night of my pilgrimage falls on the eve of the Fourth of July. I earned enough Hilton points over the last few weeks for a free stay in this final hotel. As I pulled into the parking lot, I was overwhelmed by the spectacular beauty of a breathtaking, multicolor sunset framing an American flag that was rippling in the breeze above the stone-faced building. How fitting: A grand finale on the last night of my America tour coming into the nation's birthday.

Just then it came to me. So suddenly. The same way it came to me the first time when I was at that traffic light in the little Geo Prizm back when I was just a 20-year-old young thing waiting for her child to be born. Another epiphany.

Perhaps the reason I haven't found my new reason for existing is because I'm looking too far outside myself. Perhaps I don't have to look far at all. Perhaps there's no profound external reason for my existence and it's solely and entirely for me. Perhaps there's nothing wrong with that. I get to enjoy this next stage of my life. I get to enjoy the beauties that God has given us on this earth and explore and experience and simply live. Perhaps 'myself' is my purpose.

Making the right turn off of the two-lane secondary road, I heard the familiar crunching of gravel under my tires as I maneuvered the Chevy into my driveway. I pushed the button on the ceiling of the truck to open the garage door and parked my vehicle in the familiar space. I will unload the truck in a bit.

I turned my key in the front door lock for the first time since May and the entire cylinder jiggled. I had forgotten about that, I meant to get it fixed. I made a mental note to put it on the calendar for this week. I opened my front door and my cat Oliver plodded down the steps. As he rubbed up against my leg, the sharp, high-pitched sound of his whining meow indicated that he was much more interested in a meal than in welcoming me home.

I made my way to the kitchen and opened a can of cat food, setting it in his dish on the little carpet next to the sink. I did a quick scan of my cute little apartment. Everything seemed in order. I was back.

Everything was the same. Well, it was the same, but different.